OTHER KEY CRU BOURGEOIS

CHÂTEAU CHASSE-SPLEEN

CHÂTEAU D'AGASSAC

CHÂTEAU DE PEZ

CHÂTEAU GLORIA

CHÂTEAU GREYSAC

CHÂTEAU MEYNEY

CHÂTEAU ORMES DE PEZ

CHÂTEAU PHÉLAN SÉGUR

RING THE "BELLE" FOR FIVE BORDEAUX VALUES

I have found these five lesser-known Bordeaux châteaux to consistently drink above their price. Appropriately enough, each has some variation of "belle," the French word for beautiful, in its name, so remember to ring the "belle" when you're in the Bordeaux aisle of your local wine shop.

CHÂTEAU BEL-AIR (HAUT-MÉDOC)

CHÂTEAU BELLE-VUE (HAUT-MÉDOC)

CHÂTEAU BELLEGRAVE (PAUILLAC)

CHÂTEAU BELLEVUE (ST. ÉMILION)

CHÂTEAU BELLES-GRAVES (LALANDE-DE-POMEROL)

BORDEAUX: LEFT BANK (CABERNET SAUVIGNON-DOMINATED)

BILLIONAIRE: ($1,000+)
- Château Margaux

MULTIMILLIONAIRE: ($300-$500)
- Château Cos d'Estournel
- Château Lynch-Bages
- Château Palmer

MILLIONAIRE ($150+)
- Pavillon Rouge du Château Margaux

THOUSANDAIRE ($30 to 80)
- Blason d'Issan
- Château Malescot St. Exupéry
- Château Rauzan-Ségla
- Château Siran

To avoid paying top dollar for first-rate Bordeaux, aficionados look to "second labels" of icon châteaux, such as Pavillon Rouge du Château Margaux instead of Château Margaux, which use grapes that didn't make the cut for the first label wine. Relative bargains can be also found in a category known as "Cru Bourgeois," which includes the excellent Château Siran and scores of other châteaux that didn't make the cut in the outdated Classification of 1855. Both offer the advantage of significantly gentler prices and wine that is often made with lower tannins and is thus ready to drink far sooner than the billionaire-priced wine.

BORDEAUX: RIGHT BANK (MERLOT-DOMINATED)

MULTIBILLIONAIRE ($3,000+)
- Château Pétrus

BILLIONAIRE ($1,000+)
- Château Le Pin

MULTIMILLIONAIRE ($200-$400)
- Château L'Église Clinet
- Château Trotanoy
- Vieux Châteu...

Merlot-focused Château Pétrus has long symbolized one of the world's priciest pours, but you'll pay a magnitude less for Château Trotanoy, which is also in the "Right Bank" Bordeaux appellation of Pomerol and has the same owner, the renowned Christian Moueix (pronounced "Moo-icks"). Near Pétrus is another Pomerol great, Vieux Château Certan (shortened to "VCC"); its reliance on the Cabernet Franc grape (often even more than Trotanoy) bestows on it a flavor profile somewhat different from Pétrus. In the same area are the reliable Château Le Bon Pasteur and Château de Sales, which are far less expensive, if somewhat simpler, sources of smooth, supple Right Bank magic.

OTHER KEY "SECOND LABEL" BORDEAUX

WINE	SECOND LABEL
CHÂTEAU COS D'ESTOURNEL	LES PAGODES DE COS
CHÂTEAU DUCRU-BEAUCAILLOU	LA CROIX DE BEAUCAILLOU
CHÂTEAU GRUAUD-LAROSE	SARGET DE GRUAUD-LAROSE
CHÂTEAU LAGRANGE	LES FIEFS DE LAGRANGE
CHÂTEAU LASCOMBES	CHEVALIER DE LASCOMBES
CHÂTEAU LÉOVILLE-BARTON	LA RÉSERVE DE LÉOVILLE-BARTON
CHÂTEAU LYNCH-BAGES	ECHO DE LYNCH-BAGES
CHÂTEAU PALMER	ALTER EGO DE PALMER

WHITE BURGUNDY

MULTIBILLIONAIRE ($5,000+)
- Domaine Leflaive Montrachet

BILLIONAIRE ($500 to $1500)
- Ramonet Montrachet
- Domaine Leflaive Bâtard-Montrachet
- Joseph Drouhin "Marquis de Laguiche" Montrachet

MULTIMILLIONAIRE ($200 to $500)
- Domaine Leflaive Bâtard-Montrachet
- Etienne Sauzet Chevalier-Montrachet
- Louis Jadot Bâtard-Montrachet
- Ramonet Bâtard-Montrachet

MILLIONAIRE ($60 to $120)
- Chavy-Martin Puligny-Montrachet
- Faiveley Puligny-Montrachet
- Olivier Leflaive Puligny-Montrachet
- Vincent Girardin Puligny-Montrachet "Villages Vieilles Vignes"
- Ramonet Chassagne-Montrachet

THOUSANDAIRE (Under $60)
- Dominique Lafon Bourgogne Blanc
- Faiveley Bourgogne Blanc
- Hubert Lamy St. Aubin (various)
- Olivier Leflaive Bourgogne Blanc "Les Sétilles"
- Philippe Colin St. Aubin "Le Charmois"
- Pierre-Yves Colin-Morey St. Aubin "La Chatenière"

If you'd rather avoid the prestige premium for the villages famous for Montrachet—Chassagne-Montrachet and Puligny-Montrachet—the respected appellation of St. Aubin is wedged right next to them and overdelivers for its price. Producer Pierre-Yves Colin-Morey (shortened by insiders to the ink-toner-evoking PYCM) is a blue chip for St. Aubin, as are the various vineyards of Hubert Lamy. A step down in price and, sometimes, complexity is Bourgogne blanc, which is made from grapes that can come from any part of the Burgundy region.

RED BURGUNDY

MULTIBILLIONAIRE ($5,000+)
- Domaine de la Romanée-Conti Romanée-Conti

BILLIONAIRE ($700 to $1,500+)
- Domaine Jacques-Frédéric Mugnier "Les Amoureuses" Chambolle-Musigny Premier Cru
- Domaine de la Romanée-Conti Romanée St. Vivant
- Domaine Comte Georges de Vogüé Musigny

MULTIMILLIONAIRE: ($200 to $700)
- Claude Dugat Gevrey-Chambertin Premier Cru
- Dujac Vosne-Romanée "Aux Malconsorts" Premier Cru
- G. Roumier "Les Cras" Chambolle-Musigny Premier Cru

MILLIONAIRE ($70 to 120)
- Domaine Fourrier Gevrey-Chambertin
- Dominique Mugneret Vosne-Romanée
- Jean Grivot Vosne-Romanée
- Méo-Camuzet Vosne-Romanée

THOUSANDAIRE (Under $50)
- Anne Gros Bourgogne Rouge
- Bouchard Père et Fils Bourgogne Rouge
- Champy Bourgogne Rouge
- Domaine de Montille Bourgogne Rouge
- Faiveley Bourgogne Rouge
- Henri Boillot Bourgogne Rouge
- Mugneret-Gibourg Bourgogne Rouge
- Nicolas Rossignol Bourgogne Rouge
- Sylvie Esmonin Bourgogne Rouge

It's a frustrating fact that even relatively modest Village-level Burgundy—i.e., wine made from grapes in or around a particular village—is priced beyond everyday use. If you choose carefully, however, certain village wines can drink like those of the dramatically more expensive grand cru and premier cru vineyards. Domaine Fourrier's Jean-Marie Fourrier, for example, a protégé of one of France's greatest winemakers, the late Henri Jayer, regularly makes a stunning village-level Gevrey-Chambertin. With its abundance of excellent producers, the village Chambolle-Musigny, an insider favorite, probably offers the highest quality of village-level wine, but also relatively high prices. Entry level for Burgundy is "Bourgogne," which is wine sourced not from one particular village or vineyard therein, but from grapes anywhere in the entire region of Burgundy. Bourgogne rouge is often light and simple but can be memorable in the hands of a talented winery or négociant, the latter being a producer who buys grapes from growers. Négociants such as Champy and Domaine Faiveley offer rewarding quality at surprisingly palatable prices.

HOW TO PLAY DRC, THE WORLD'S MOST COVETED PRODUCER

A way to spend hundreds instead of thousands for the wine of Domaine de la Romanée-Conti is to fin a bottle of its Vosne-Romanée "Cuvée Duvault-Blochet," which is made from leftover grapes from the young vines of some of DRC's legendary *cru* vineyards. If you do long to try of DRC's fabled *gran crus* but can't quite stomach the vertiginously priced Romanée-Conti La Tâche, you would do well t consider the *Grand Cru* Romanée-Saint-Vivant, which is located a stone's throw from those famous vineyards. The RSV is still priced for billionaires, but because it is less known and more recently und the domaine's control, it isn't quite as depleting. In some years, I prefer this delicate, fragrant charm to the more expensive and renowned Romanée-Conti La Tâche.

AFFORDABLE RED BURGUNDY IS NOT OXYMORONIC

Being a tiny region coveted by connoisseurs for what many consider the world's best Pinot Noir, it i no surprise that red Burgundy is punishingly expensive. There is hope, however. In addition to bett bottles at the Bourgogne rouge level, I lean on the three less-heralded areas of Burgundy listed belo for light-bodied, earthy, and sometimes compellingly good red Burgundy. With wines from Burgundy varying widely by producer, vintage, and particular vineyards, always try to consult a truste merchant or sommelier to confirm that a specific bottle will be to your taste.

MARSANNAY: Bart, Chanson, Louis Latour, Domaine Joseph et Philippe Roty, Trapet
SAVIGNY-LÈS-BEAUNE: Maurice Ecard, Simon Bize, Jean-Marc Pavelot, Nicolas Rossignol, Tollot-Bea
PERNAND-VERGELESSES: Chandon de Briailles, Chanson, Mongeard-Mugneret, Rapet, Rollin

HOW TO DRINK LIKE A BILLIONAIRE

MASTERING WINE
WITH JOIE DE VIVRE

HOW TO DRINK
LIKE A BILLIONAIRE

MASTERING WINE
WITH JOIE DE VIVRE

UB.

Batch No. 300   256 Pages   **MARK OLDMAN**   750 ml   14.5% Vol

REGAN ARTS · NEW YORK
CUVÉE RARE

Regan
Arts.
65 BLEECKER STREET
NEW YORK, NY 10012

FOR INFORMATION, ADDRESS REGAN ARTS SUBSIDIARY RIGHTS DEPARTMENT, 65 BLEECKER STREET, NEW YORK, NY 10012.

IMAGE CREDITS, WHICH CONSTITUTE AN EXTENSION OF THIS COPYRIGHT PAGE, APPEAR ON PAGE 244.

FIRST REGAN ARTS HARDCOVER EDITION, OCTOBER 2016.

LIBRARY OF CONGRESS CONTROL NUMBER: 2016932846

COPYRIGHT © 2016
BY MARK OLDMAN

JACKET DESIGN BY
STEVE ATTARDO / NINETYNORTH DESIGN

INTERIOR DESIGN BY
STEVE ATTARDO / NINETYNORTH DESIGN

INTERIOR ILLUSTRATIONS BY
JOEL HOLLAND

10 9 8 7 6 5 4 3 2 1

ISBN 978-1-942872-14-6

Printed in China

"WE ARE ALL MORTAL
UNTIL THE FIRST KISS
AND THE SECOND GLASS
OF WINE."

—EDUARDO GALEANO,

URUGUAYAN JOURNALIST

AND WRITER

CONTENTS

CONTENTS CTD....

CONTENTS CTD. . . .

Seul Concessionnaire pour la France: Marcellin FIORIO à LÉZIGNAN (Aude)

CONTENTS CTD....

CONTENTS CTD....

GRAND CRU CLASSÉ EN 1855

CHÂTEAU

BRANE-CANTENAC

NAN (Aude)

ANNÉE 2006

INTRODUCTION

NO. <u>0001</u>

Mise en Bouteille au Domaine

13% ALC. BY VOL   PRODUCT OF NEW YORK   750 ML

As we ambled away from the discount warehouse in Sunnyvale, California, giddy from an excess of free samples and the acquisition of underpriced wine, the realization struck me: contrary to prevailing belief, even billionaires do not want to spend recklessly on wine.

I was with my friend Diane, an elegant, down-to-earth woman whose family has made unfathomable riches in Silicon Valley. She is one of the numerous billionaires I've met who manages to make smart choices about wine. Keenly appreciative of how easy it is lose it all, the billionaires I know tend to focus their energies on the preservation of their wealth.

So in my experience, the superrich are surprisingly careful when ordering wine in restaurants—all too aware of how difficult it is to find value there. They cultivate relationships with good merchants. They understand how to cut through sales patter and gain satisfying returns on their liquid assets. They uncover what insiders are drinking. And many billionaires are unafraid to circumvent the pretention and geekiness that still surrounds so much of wine.

But the fact remains: you don't have to be a billionaire to drink like one.

As I sipped on a glass of cut-price D.P. from Costco, my mission crystallized like a Swarovski necklace: I would teach everyone how to drink like a billionaire. No, this is not something that necessitates spending like an incautious oligarch. In many instances, it is quite the opposite.

Drinking like a billionaire means imbibing like someone completely in control, like someone fully in the know or a mere text message away from it.

And so we have this book. In it, you will learn to approach wine like a shrewd member of the one percent, covering how to:

CONSERVE CASH

Billionaires will, of course, spend for special occasion wines, but they rarely order from the reserve list. They are often happiest with moderately priced bottles that drink above their cost. Therefore, we'll explore ways to maximize your enjoyment of wine without spending more than you have to, including addressing the threshold concept that price is not proportional to quality (chapter 1), dismissing the notion that you need several glass types (chapter 61), and exploring how to use a critic's points to your economic advantage (chapter 89).

DRINK LIKE AN INSIDER

The super rich are ahead of the game when it comes learning what the cognoscenti are doing. So we are going to cover key maneuvers such as how to swirl wine for maximum effect (chapter 6), which wine flaws to overlook (chapter 71), and how to find what I call a "wine spouse" (chapter 87).

BREAK THE RULES

Billionaires don't want to waste their time or sacrifice their pleasure for the sake of outdated or useless rules. Like the iconoclastic winemakers that are so

popular today, they are mavericks at heart, with no compunction about dropping ice in wine (chapter 64), drinking red wine with fish (chapter 23), and experimenting with surprisingly delicious food and wine pairings (chapter 36).

AVOID GETTING "BANGED" BY A BAD SOMM
We will cover innovative ways to identify and defend against a "bad somm" (chapter 51), how to spot a dark-hearted wine merchant (chapter 84), why you should giggle at overly specific food and wine matches (chapter 21), and even techniques to guard against overzealous pourers and bottle stranders (chapter 59).

HOME IN ON THE BEST VALUES
Billionaires know how to cut through the chaos and cherry-pick the best-valued options that suit their taste. With wine from every conceivable region now flooding the market, nowhere is such discernment more important than in wine selection. I have thus painstakingly assembled Oldman's Ten Best lists (section 3), which distill my twenty-six years of teaching wine into carefully considered rankings of wine types organized by taste preference.

AVOID DOUCHE-DOM
You know that braggadocio spouting off about wine or giving the waiter a hard time? She's not the billionaire. The billionaire is the one in the corner, ready to wield her quiet power. Let the poseur or grandstander make a scene; the billionaire will dare to say nothing (chapter 9) or, if warranted, will know exactly how to send a wine back (chapter 69) or return it to a store (chapter 86).

DRINK WITH STYLE
If the infinitely moneyed are cool, it is on their own terms. Think of a drinker who embodies the élan of Richard Branson or Oprah Winfrey. They know how to avoid being slaves to wine trends (chapter 78), when to sniff but not sip a wine (chapter 55), what smelling an empty glass signals (chapters 14 and 60), and, of course, they know how to decapitate a frothy bottle of Champagne (chapter 114).

TALK THE TALK
Good billionaires radiate savoir faire—whether it means knowing the insider lingo that rarely makes it into any blog (chapter 102), cool little French expressions for wine (chapter 103), or the most creative way to convey a good buzz. But they also know how to spot the empty pontification favored by certain wine authorities (chapter 89).

GIVE GOOD GIFTS
The ultrarich know that while gifts do not necessarily need to be expensive, they should always be perceived as special. This is why I detail how and why to buy a meaningful vintage (chapter 95), wines never to give as gifts (chapter 100), and why Champagne is the perfect present for a newborn (chapter 96).

DUNK COOKIES IN WINE
Most of the billionaires I know are unapologetic about their own enjoyment and that of those around them. Confident enough to ignore the smug evangelists and killjoys who beleaguer wine culture, they won't hesitate to dunk cookies in wine (chapter 33), drizzle wine on dessert (chapter 34), pour from big bottles

(chapter 93), and even add a recreational Breathalyzer (chapter 113) or Spanish porron to the mix (chapter 112).

The ethos of this book is a logical next step following the success of my Wine for Billionaires seminars at the Aspen Food & Wine Classic, as well as similarly themed events I conduct at my Manhattan home, which I call the "wine sanctuary." And it is informed by my work advising high-net-worth clients on their collections and for special events.

Finally, do not confuse the billionaire perspective of this book with the encouragement of snobbery. From my original Anti-Snob Wine Seminars and my first two wine books, *Oldman's Guide to Outsmarting Wine* and *Oldman's Brave New World of Wine,* to countless appearances at the country's top food festivals and the dozens of articles I've penned for major publications, I strive to puncture pomposity and encourage people of all capacities to "drink bravely." As anyone who has spent time with me will attest, I relish deeply the chance to relieve drinkers of wine's pretentiousness. It is in this spirit that we shall now, with an insider eye and a flavorful dollop of fun, drink richly.

PART

FUNDAM

750 ML

ONE

ENTALS

20% Alc. By Vol.

1 PLEASURE IS NOT PROPORTIONAL TO PRICE

Contrary to common belief, paying more doesn't necessarily get you tastier wine. Price can indeed reflect a wine's quality, meaning that more dollars will often increase the likelihood that the juice comes from better grapes handled by skillful winemakers. There's no guarantee, however, that such virtue will translate to a taste that you will find superior. And even if it does, after a certain price point—as low as $20 for some wine types—you are likely paying less for the wine's intrinsic quality and more for other things.

Where do those extra dollars go? Sometimes you are paying for the scarcity of a wine made in small quantities. Or you are subsidizing a winery's glossy advertisements, beach umbrellas, or branded baby bibs. Some wines are priced higher simply to get consumers to value them more. A recent study at Stanford Business School confirmed this effect, finding that subjects registered more pleasure in their brain when they were told a wine was costlier. If that does not convince you about the sometimes tenuous connection between wine price and quality, know that I will often have my students blind-taste two wines and then guess the expensive one. More often than not, at least half of the audience—even the long-standing connoisseurs—get it wrong.

Pleasure vs. Price

2 DON'T JUDGE A WINE BY ITS FIRST SIP

Most of us know how to taste wine from the restaurant ritual, the self-conscious moment in which we check wine for "off" smells. After your waiter pours a taste, you swirl, sniff, and decide.

That is all well and good for sampling a wine for faults, but I implore you not to judge the overall taste of wine like that. I have had innumerable wines that start unspectacularly, only to change for the better after a few minutes.

Actually, sometimes it is you, and your powers of perception, that makes the transformation. Your palate needs time to get over that Listerine strip from an hour ago or the forty-clove garlic chicken that tattooed itself on your tongue at lunch. Or maybe you became rattled by the deeply untalented mariachi band playing near your table, since the enjoyment of wine is often contextual. A wine's taste changes with one's surroundings; why else would so many people enjoy a wine more on vacation than they would enjoy another bottle of it back home in the daily grind? Moreover, food can dramatically alter your perception of wine. For example, an astringent Barolo will taste less bitter in the presence of proteins like steak and fats such as cheese.

Sometimes the wine itself needs to come around. An agricultural product, wine evolves in your glass as it is exposed to air, becoming more expressive and a bit softer, and more so when it is placed in a decanter (chapter 67). Even in cases for which there is an initial whiff of a worrisome element like sulfur, for example, that flaw can, in wine parlance, "blow off" with time, revealing a delicious wine underneath.

So although it is true that during a job interview or on a hot date you never get a second chance to make a first impression, it is best to give your wine more time before drawing a conclusion. Linger with it, and learn.

3 PRACTICE VINOUS PROMISCUITY

Everything is different now. Ambitious new generations of winemakers and vastly improved technology are revitalizing forgotten grapes and revamping wine regions around the world. Supported by an increasingly passionate cadre of sommeliers and wine merchants, the consumer now has a broad and multifarious array of wine choice.

But few of us are taking full advantage of it. Even practicing oenophiles tend to channel their energies into just a few silos, be it Sancerre or Sonoma Pinot Noir. This is understandable: wine's relative expense tends to discourage experimentation, and it wasn't that long ago that choice was far more limited.

Why be promiscuous with your loyalties? At the least, exposing yourself to new wine types will help you find affordable and more interesting alternatives to the styles of wine you already like. Already a confirmed Pinot-phile? Try Beaujolais or Bourgueil or any of the other alternatives I lovingly detail in section 3. They are waiting for your discovery like juicy plums in a crate.

Even better, exploration will open your eyes to styles you didn't think you liked. All it takes is one disappointment to dismiss a category forever, yet you would be astonished to know how many of my students swear off a wine like Sauvignon Blanc or Rioja only to eventually fall for it when they finally find a good one.

Vinous promiscuity is self-perpetuating. Once you get in the groove of trying new wines, you find yourself searching for others. You may even do so in hopes of eventually visiting the vineyard in person. It is no accident that some of the world's most dazzling destinations are wine zones. Wine discovery, in fact, is the ultimate escape from our overly connected world. It is a lifelong avocation that welcomes company and requires no exertion beyond the hoisting of a glass to your lips.

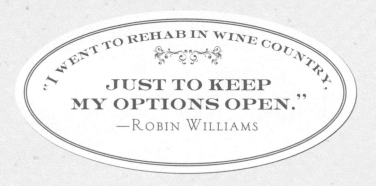

"I WENT TO REHAB IN WINE COUNTRY,

JUST TO KEEP MY OPTIONS OPEN."

—ROBIN WILLIAMS

4 EMBRACE THE BUZZ

One of the most curious aspects of wine appreciation is how little attention is given to its most prominent effect: that warm feeling of elevation you get from it; in other words, the buzz. We can wax rhapsodic about wine's velvety texture, talk endlessly about its notes of tomato leaves and gooseberries, and bore the dog about reverse osmosis and gravity feeds. But speak fondly of its intoxicating impact, and it clears a room like fusion jazz at a junior prom. Ignoring wine's heightening effects is to me tantamount to a car enthusiast neglecting the thrill of speed: it misses a key point of the enterprise.

Don't get me wrong, I am not singing the praises of Hemingway-esque fits of self-destructive excess. I am not endorsing the kind of serial inebriation or Falstaffian binge drinking that generates all sorts of problems. I am talking about using wine to achieve that feeling of well-being, that glow of pleasure, that rush of experience that comes with enjoying a few glasses of something really satisfying.

In her no-nonsense book, *Buzzed,* even Duke University physician Cynthia Kuhn acknowledges alcohol's ability to promote feelings of well-being and "activate pleasure circuits."

More poetically, it is what English writer John Milton meant when he wrote of wine's ability to "bathe the drooping spirits in delight." And we are not just talking about a state of happiness. Wine has the ability to spark the mind and, for some, awake genius. An array of writers and artists has testified to wine's link to imaginative transcendence. Hemingway himself advised one to "write drunk, edit sober."

Perhaps the buzz of wine is best viewed as an escape chute from the burdens of modern life. In a glass or two, wine accomplishes what so many meditation tapes and seminars promise. It makes you comfortably numb, takes you outside of yourself to experience, however briefly, a heightened, less onerous perspective. The ancient philosopher Seneca once wrote about how the statesman Cato used wine to soothe his mind when it was "tired from the cares of state." Almost two thousand years later in his book *Vintage,* wine writer Hugh Johnson compared the beauty of a rose to that of wine, noting that only the latter has the power to "banish care." Or as I printed on a button for my seminars (against the advice of my concerned psychologist mom): "Feelings Hurt. Wine Helps."

APPREC

PART

1

WIIII

PRODI

Mis

s.a.r.l Olga Raffault "Ra

1,5 ALC./VOL.

IATION
DEUX

23 ————————————————

RE WINE

FRANCE

lle par
7 420 Savigny en Veron

750 ML.

5 DOUBLE FIST TO UNDERSTAND DIFFERENCES

If I asked you to choose between two paintings or two perfumes, you would be in the best position to judge them when the items were placed side by side. Nowhere is the need for such comparative discernment greater than in the appreciation of wine, where differences are subtle and the stimulus for the senses is short-lived. The problem, however, is that most of our imbibing is done sequentially, whether at a restaurant or home. You drink one wine, and then, thirst willing, you might move on to another. Even the lineup of tastes available at some bars and seminars—so-called wine flights—aren't particularly conducive to parsing the differences among wines, because we end up drinking sequentially. By the time you progress to your next wine, your smell and taste memory of the previous one has often faded.

My technique to appreciate the subtleties of a wine is to go back and forth, with briskness and determination, between two wines. For this, it is helpful to double fist, assigning one glass to each hand. Can't understand how wine is supposed to smell earthy or oaky or redolent of asparagus? Or don't taste how a wine is supposed to be light or tangy or sweet? Sniff and sip it against another wine. Go back and forth between the wines a few times.

At some point during this comparative process, distinctions become easier to see. That peppery quality in one or those floral notes in the other start to emerge—even if you never considered yourself a particularly perceptive drinker. It may not be the most elegant way to enjoy your wine, but using a glass in each hand and comparing the two—I call it "vinodexterity"—is a powerful maneuver to suss out the nuances hidden in wine.

6 CURB THY SWIRL

Do you give good swirl? Clockwise or vice versa? In the air? On the table? I am happy to hear it, because giving your wine a whirl will aerate it, releasing its vapors and allowing you to smell more things in it. You may detect aromas of fruit or flowers or spice or perhaps more exotic things like baked bread or minerals; almost anything is fair game when appreciating a wine's aromas, collectively known to tasters as its "nose."

While this taster's twitch is so fundamental to wine appreciation that it is generally taught in the first minutes of Wine 101, the problem comes when drinkers become lost to the swirl.

What starts as a legitimate technique to aerate the wine can devolve into any number of elliptical transgressions. Some swirl too aggressively, orbiting their wine like some frenzied act of self-gratification. Others operate their glass with unfortunate hauteur in a desperate attempt at identifying themselves with some imaginary society of pinkie lifters.

Then there are those who focus so much on their swirl that it alienates those around them, not unlike a tablemate obsessed with their smartphone. A person can become so addicted to the swirl that they absentmindedly swirl everything on the table—their water glass, the flower vase, or the votive candle.

Whatever the occasion, it is best to give your wine a quick, crisp swirl, take a few deliberate inhalations, and then taste it. You will get a good read of the wine without shedding friends and infuriating people.

7 SWIRL WITH A LID

A common concern I hear from wine enthusiasts is that they cannot smell much in their wine. Sometimes it is the wine's fault: certain grapes, such as quotidian renditions of Pinot Grigio or Prosecco, tend to have a dull neutrality, the aroma equivalent of your friends' vacation photos or a TED talk on the uses of zinc.

Sometimes blame goes to a wineglass whose bowl isn't large enough to concentrate the wine's vapors; size counts for a lot in wineglasses (chapter 61). Or we ourselves are at fault, failing to swirl briskly and then sniff deeply with one's nose well into the glass—being mindful, of course, not to overdo it. We can also sabotage matters by wearing an excess of fragrance, lotion, or deodorant, all of which can obscure a wine's aromas.

The solution is a tool that requires neither purchase nor preparation: your hand. Most of us are already used to using our hands to wave in good fragrances and ward off the malodorous ones. Here, you close your hand over the top of the glass as if you were trapping a firefly. Now swirl your glass with your other hand while keeping the seal up top with the other. I call this "lidding" the glass, and by doing so, you trap in the vapors as the wine spins and you get a much more concentrated hit of the wine. Then uncover the glass and sniff like you mean it. The effect is like turning up the volume on the wine's bouquet.

8 WINE IS NOT MOUTHWASH

Overswirling may be socially perilous, but worse is the misguided advice that drinkers should vigorously aerate wine in their mouths. After you sniff your wine, the common directive goes, take the wine into your mouth and suck in air to make the flavors more pronounced. Gargle and chew your wine. Slosh it against the sides of your mouth. Make noises like Hannibal Lecter contemplating liver, fava beans, and a nice Chianti.

Although this motorboating technique can be helpful to accentuate a wine's flavors by causing its volatile elements to vaporize, it is really only necessary for professionals when they evaluate wine at trade events and competitions. Putting aside its ridiculous, self-important appearance, slurping isn't recommended because it can often lead to choking and dribbling, thereby imperiling your clothing. Crucially, it doesn't remove any of the limitations of what is the less sensitive of your two senses. We can taste just five elements—sweet, sour, bitter, salty, and savory/umami—whereas we can sniff thousands of things, making the nose far more sensitive to the finer nuances of wine.

This should not discourage you from getting a good, evaluative taste of the wine. Take a healthy sip and see if you can evaluate the wine for its weight or body (light, medium, or full?), acidity (low, moderate, or tartly sharp?), and dryness (bone-dry, off-dry, or sweet?), and with red wine, its level of tannin (low, moderate, or gum-dryingly high?). But you had best leave any gargling and burbling to coffee machines and heating pipes.

9 DARE TO SAY NOTHING

It was several years into my wine journey when I figured out a vital lesson from my friend Burt, a renowned wine collector and a paragon of vinous generosity. He has uncorked thousands of priceless bottles for his friends and family, but when he does, he says scarcely anything about these rare specimens. He might tell you where they are from, a bit why they are special, but he never issues grocery lists or other such braggadocious bluster that alienates novices and many connoisseurs, too.

This is because he knows something that some drinkers never quite get: most people, even oenophiles, don't want to hear it. Grape nuts solely in the company of one another, of course, should feel free, if they wish, to exchange impressions like anime fanboys at Comic Con. And learning and using vocabulary about wine is essential to communicate your preferences to those serving and selling wine. I even think that knowing some rhapsodically obscure and hyperbolic wine words (chapter 102) can be useful for a laugh or to put a blowhard in his place.

But in the company of most sentient human beings, wine pontification traumatizes. There is a fine, elusive line between know-your-stuff and know-it-all. Journalist Calvin Trilling in an essay on Slate.com showed keen insight when he suggested that those who talk a lot about wine have no less than a 61 percent ACI (asshole correlation index).

Not only that, excess wine speak can bias others' own perception of a wine, and that is another reason why some of the most gracious connoisseurs bite their tongues: to allow others to form their own impressions. As a New York gallery owner once said of how best to appreciate art: listen well, look long, and speak little.

10 LEGS ARE EMINENTLY IGNORABLE

You know there just had to be a patient zero for the syndrome of talking about a wine's legs—that is, somewhere, years ago, one person was to blame for spreading the mistaken belief that legs signify quality. I wonder if that first legs-lusting oenophile had any idea what worldwide confusion and wasted effort he would cause.

These days, legs—which are the droplets that trickle down the side of a glass after you swirl wine—are largely ignored, although some novices still fall victim to the myth of their significance. What legs reflect is alcohol content, such that noticeable droplets—so-called good legs—can indicate a wine of relatively high alcohol, but there are too many exceptions for it to be consistently illuminating.

If your tablemates just *have* to discuss legs, all is not lost. While you are dissuading them from the notion that legs have oenological import, you can display your poetic side by using the captivating word "rivulet" (that is, a small stream of liquid) as well as invoking legs' many lyrical synonyms like "tears," "fingers," "curtains," "candles," and "church windows." You can also exercise your inner illusionist by showing what happens when you spin a glass of wine with your other hand covering it: the evaporation of alcohol ceases, causing any legs to magically disappear.

COMPONENTS

NO. <u>0002</u>

Mise en Bouteille au Domaine

11 YOU'RE NOT THINKING ENOUGH ABOUT TEXTURE

I f the casual drinker is not used to taking stock of a wine's smell and taste, the consideration of texture is even less familiar. Outside of evil dental needles, canker sores, and curiously strong mints, we do not pay heed to the stimuli on our gums, tongue, and palate.

Yet you are probably familiar with wine's more obvious tactile sensations when you feel them. There is wine's "body," which is how heavy it feels in your mouth. The commonly used analogy equates light-bodied wine with water, medium body with skim milk, and a full body with whole milk or cream.

Then there are other textural components that you have likely come across in a wine class or article. Alcohol (chapter 16) can manifest itself as a "hot" sensation on the palate when it is in ample proportions. Tannins can create a puckering dryness in your mouth, while acidity often tingles on your tongue, the difference between the two are often confused and thus worthy of elaboration ahead (chapter 12).

The magic of wine, however, often comes in noticing the overall sensation that wine renders on your mouth. Consider a glass of Champagne: are the bubbles small and finely knit on your tongue, or are they large and ungainly like a slurp of Schweppes? Does a Meursault create a creamy, almost oily feel on your tongue, a rich slipperiness that makes you feel all funny inside? Does a delicate Pinot Noir paint your tongue with a silky, satiny smoothness? Does a rich Barossa Shiraz envelop your gums in a powdery mist? Does that young Barolo rule your mouth with the hurt-so-good roughness of a dominatrix's boot? Use your tongue, and your mind, to think more about texture in these ways.

12 KNOW YOUR TINGLE FROM YOUR PUCKER

Understanding the difference between acidity and tannin is key to wine tasting, but most resources fail to differentiate these two textural sensations head-on. Let's get to it.

Acidity, perhaps the most important single component in wine, is the tingle you feel on your tongue and inner cheeks. Present in both red and white wine, it tends to be most apparent in zingy styles of white wine, such as Sauvignon Blanc and Riesling, but it is also an essential feature in food-friendly reds. It is the primary reason why we perceive some wines as fresh, lively, and vibrant, and it also provides an essential counterbalance to the sweetness of off-dry and dessert wines.

Like a lemon squeeze on a salmon fillet, acidity provides lift to food, heightening flavors and cutting through richness. It also invigorates the appetite and refreshes the mouth, preparing your mouth for the next bite. Because the term "acidity" conjures up something that necessitates a fistful of Tums or burns through laboratory floors, people like to euphemistically refer to it as a wine's crispness, tanginess, or, at the extreme, tartness. How much acidity you like in your wine is a personal preference, but too little is considered flabby and dull, while too much can rattle your teeth.

Tannin, on the other hand, is the dry, puckering sensation you feel in your mouth. In addition to being in tea and leather, tannin is a compound that resides in the skins, seeds, and stems of grapes. Because red wine, unlike white, spends more time in contact with its skins, tannin tends to show in certain red wines, especially thick-skinned types like Cabernet Sauvignon and Syrah. In moderate proportions, tannin can provide a pleasantly dry feeling that gives a wine oomph and sometimes the ability to get better with age. It can also help impart that smooth, powdery, or velvety sensation that we feel in some reds. When excessive, it is lip-strippingly, gum-numbingly bitter, making a wine literally hard to swallow. The solution for highly tannic wines is to drink them with protein-rich foods such as cheeses and meats, which, like milk in tea, will tone down your perception of tannin.

Walnuts, tea, Red Wine are all in the Thrall of Tannin. a Puckering griper on the Tongue and gums Mistress Tannin turns the scen Astringently yours ...but sometimes Softer she envelopes with silken finesse, a Velvet Caress Lends an Oomph to dishes ageability to wine lessening in time a fair feline this Leathery Dominatrix Whose Boot is so fine

ACIDITY VS. TANNIN FACE-OFF

SYMBOL
ACIDITY: LEMON | TANNIN: TEA

MAKES A WINE...
ACIDITY: FRESH, VIBRANT | TANNIN: DRY, PUCKERING

MANIFESTS IN MOUTH AS...
ACIDITY: TINGLE | TANNIN: PUCKER

SALIVA
ACIDITY: STIMULATES IT | TANNIN: STEALS IT

FUNCTION
ACIDITY: HEIGHTENS FLAVOR, CUTS RICHNESS, BALANCES SWEETNESS, SOMETIMES ENABLES AGEABILITY | TANNIN: ADDS TEXTURE, CONTRIBUTES TO AGEABILITY

EASIER IDENTIFIED IN...
ACIDITY: WHITE WINE | TANNIN: RED WINE

PARADIGMATIC WINE
ACIDITY: SAUVIGNON BLANC | TANNIN: CABERNET SAUVIGNON

IN EXCESS
ACIDITY: ELECTRICITY, BUZZING | TANNIN: SANDPAPER, DUSTY

METAPHORICAL DESTINATION
ACIDITY: ELECTRIC TOWER | TANNIN: SAHARA DESERT

METAPHORICAL BEVERAGE
ACIDITY: LEMONADE | TANNIN: OVERLY CONCENTRATED TEA, ESPRESSO

SADOMASOCHISTIC TERM
ACIDITY: PRICKLY | TANNIN: CHAFING

FANCY WORD
ACIDITY: ASTRINGENT | TANNIN: SCABROUS

INSIDER TERM
ACIDITY: NERVY (FOR HOW IT JUMPS ON THE TONGUE) | TANNIN: GRIPPY (FOR HOW IT GRIPS THE PALATE)

ANTHROPOMORPHIC TERM
ACIDITY: VIVACIOUS, SOUR | TANNIN: MUSCULAR, HARD

CAN BE MODERATED SOMEWHAT BY...
ACIDITY: ACIDIC OR SALTY FOOD | TANNIN: FAT AND PROTEINS, DECANTING

13 OAK CAN BE DELIGHTFULLY SLUTTY

Certain foods are slutty. They just are. Paella, with its crispy, sweating rice, is slutty. Spanish shrimp dredged in garlicky oil—slutty. Yorkshire pudding—not slutty. Chicken tikka masala—temptingly creamy, but somehow not slutty. Neither is a hot dog, though it can be deeply satisfying. Oysters—more sexy than slutty. Garlic bread—very slutty. The Middle Eastern sumac-and-sesame spice called za'atar—exotically slutty like a wild-eyed belly dancer. Soup dumplings' piping-hot, shirt-staining porkiness—sadistically slutty.

Oak in wine can be slutty, but not always. When it is in the right proportion, a wine's contact with oak barrels adds a creamy, vanilla-tinged dimension to a wine, whether white or red. Too much oak can weigh a wine down and obscure the fruit flavors that naturally come from the grape—turning what would be a fine whiff of apples or raspberries or flowers into a cloud of vanilla deodorizer

WHAT IS SLUTTY?

NOT SLUTTY	SLUTTY
WILD RICE	PAELLA
SHRIMP COCKTAIL	SHRIMPS IN GARLIC (QAMBAS)
JELLY	PEANUT BUTTER
PUMPERNICKEL BREAD	GARLIC BREAD
SUNFLOWER SEEDS	PUMPKIN SEEDS
CHICKEN	CHICKEN AND WAFFLES
DIJON MUSTARD	BÉARNAISE SAUCE
BEANS	BAKED BEANS
BUTTERED SPINACH	CREAMED SPINACH
TIRAMISU	BAKLAVA
OREGANO	ZA'ATAR

SEEMINGLY SLUTTY, BUT NOT	QUIETLY SLUTTY, LIKE A SEXY LIBRARIAN
COTTON CANDY	AVOCADOS
HAMBURGER	BEETS
PIZZA	STRAWBERRY ICE CREAM
CANDY CORN	COUSCOUS
BOTTLED SALAD DRESSING	AIRPLANE FOOD
NUTELLA	
PORK LOIN	
WHIPPED CREAM	
DUCK FAT	
LASAGNA	

or smoky cedar. It can also make wine hard to pair with food by steamrolling the flavor of delicate preparations.

This is why the general trend in winemaking is to pull back on the use of oak where it was previously used more liberally. It is fair to say that your average Californian Chardonnay or Shiraz from Australia has toned down its oakiness, though many versions remain noticeably oaky, some unapologetically so.

And why shouldn't they? So many people still have a hedonistic regard for the hand of oak. I myself often gravitate toward leaner, refreshing wines of restrained oak, but there is still a place in my heart for creamy, nutmeg- or smoke-shaded, slutty, old-school, oaky Chardonnay or Cabernet, especially when it has enough fruit flavor and acidity to balance out its oak.

Ultimately, you have to ask who you would rather hang out with: are you the person who derives occasional pleasure from big oaky wines as they would a frothing vanilla milk shake, or someone who reflexively scoffs at oak because they heard that the cool kids in wine no longer consider it vinously correct?

Oysters: more sexy than slutty

14 CONSIDER THY EMPTY GLASS

One of the fundamentals of appreciating wine is to consider its "finish," or persisting aftertaste in your mouth. Everyday wines often evaporate off your palate after five or ten seconds, while a commanding wine has enjoyable flavors that will echo on your palate for thirty seconds or longer, like a song that resonates with you after the music has ended.

While most enthusiasts focus on aftertaste, not many think to consider the lingering vapors a great wine leaves in your empty glass once the wine is gone. Pick up the glass and breathe in. Tilt it back and forth. Are the wine's aromas still emanating from the glass? A great wine will haunt your glass. And unlike the distraction of slurping wine, this is something you can do without calling too much attention to yourself and exasperating your tablemates.

Nosing your empty glass enlarges your wine experience by gleaning more information from the wine. Sometimes it is not until you linger with your empty glass that you finally detect that hint of butterscotch or black pepper that someone else noticed earlier. And it is not only unctuous, glass-coating wine that leaves an afterglow; the traces of even a delicate wine drift up from the glass like a vaporous halo.

Another benefit of lingering with your empty glass is that it elongates the sensory pleasure you receive from the wine. In our frazzled, overstimulated culture, we rarely get a moment to meditate with soul-stirring aromas. Close your eyes, relax, and relish the present. What this amounts to is unplanned aromatherapy and mindfulness—something we would all do well to take whenever we can get them.

HOW TO
QUIETLY SHOW YOUR GUN

There is another use for the empty glass, but it comes at the *beginning* of the meal. When the waiter sets down your glass, give its empty bowl a few brisk, deliberate sniffs. Insiders do this to ensure that no impurities, like residual dishwasher soap, are on the glass. Like an undercover cop who lets people glimpse the Glock 19 in his waistband, this maneuver commands instant respect.

NEW YORK — 2016 — NEW YORK

15 THE OVERRIDING FACTOR IN GREAT WINE

Experts love to debate the factors that make a wine transcendent, which can be a fool's errand given the subjectivity inherent in aesthetic determinations. What makes an artwork or recipe a masterpiece?

While the answer for wine can be elusive, there are actually factors that many experts agree on. The most common is the idea of "balance," such that an exceptional wine won't have any one element—fruit, tannin, or acidity—out of proportion. Such a wine is considered "harmonious" with all of its features "well-integrated." You might even call it "seamless." Another common qualification for greatness is "complexity," which means that a wine possesses a range of intriguing aromas and tastes rather than just one or two notes. The more poetic among us liken complexity to a kaleidoscope or to the fanning out of a peacock's tail. And what good are these layers if they do not endure? So we also look for the length of a wine's finish.

Many of the best wines I have had manage another quality: intensity of flavor without heaviness on the palate. Like a person who is both wise *and* humorous, the rare instance of a wine being both powerful and seemingly weightless is the Venn diagram overlap of greatness. The best examples of red Burgundy, for example, display this rare equipoise.

Finally, if I had to identify one overriding attribute common to every sublime wine that has passed my lips, it is simply this: Does it create a craving? In other words, does the wine compel you to want more as you are drinking it? Can you take it or leave it, or does it make you yearn for another sip? Ask yourself, is it compulsively craveable? So for me the ultimate measure of wine relates to the feeling it arouses in you. The difference between a merely good wine and a spellbinding one is similar to what makes a musical composition uncommonly special: it creates the urgent need for more.

PART-

HOW TO DRINK LIKE A BILL
PRODUCT

WINE

2010
VINTAGE

PRODUCED A
ESTVAN ATTA

HREE

RE - PART 3 - WINE TYPES
NEW YORK

TYPES

BOTTLED BY
O WINES CO.

3/4 QUARTS
12% Alc. BY VOLUME

OLDMAN'S
10 BEST

NO. 0003

Mise en Bouteille au Domaine

13% ALC. BY VOL   **PRODUCT OF NEW YORK**   750 ML

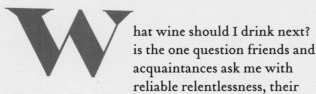

hat wine should I drink next? is the one question friends and acquaintances ask me with reliable relentlessness, their voices desperate and searching as if they were cornering a physician for advice at a cocktail party. I respond by asking what type of wine they prefer: white or red, light or rich? I also inquire: is it an everyday or special occasion purchase? Once I know this, I slide them recommendations that spring from my many years of teaching wine.

This section aims to provide you with a similar experience. I want you to feel like I am sitting across from you, clueing you in on the best of what I know and sparing you the sales pitches and technical jargon that often saddles wine discovery. This is where I provide you with pithy, need-to-know nuggets about the wine types that have consistently offered the most pleasure to my students and me.

To think through each kind of wine and come up with a defensible ranking, I considered dozens of categories through the prism of what I call the L-RAP method, ranking each wine type according to:

LIKABILITY:

How easily and often does the wine type please the majority of my students and me? Like abstract art, does it take effort to see its greatness, or is no convincing required?

RELIABILITY:

How consistent is the wine across producers? How important is it to find just the right winery or do many do the wine justice?

AVAILABILITY:

How easy is it to find the wine in restaurants and shops?

PRICE:

Do bottles generally fall into the $15 to $25 sweet spot at retail (see chapter 78), or are they remarkably inexpensive or dispiritingly costly?

Assigning each L-RAP factor a score from 1 (low) to 5 (high) enabled me to give each wine type a composite score. The rankings then fell into place: categories that scored higher ranked above those that didn't. Major types that aren't mentioned, such as Pinotage from South Africa or Chasselais from Switzerland, aren't necessarily undeserving of your consideration. It is just that some combination of the four factors— e.g., the wine is too much of an acquired taste or too pricey or inconsistent across producers or unusually difficult to source— made them score lower than the others. Ranking something as subjective as wine is not supposed to be the final word on these types; I'm aware people have differing tastes in wine, like they do in music, pizza, and manscaping. You might not agree with all of my choices, but I hope that my candid and methodical approach inspires you to find additional options that fit your taste. You can then use a trusted sommelier, merchant, or technology to zero in on specific producers. With a little luck, you may even find your new spirit wine.

OLDMAN'S 10 BEST
Alternatives to Pinot Grigio

The Pinot Gris grape from northern Italy: famous, ubiquitous, and often-times as moving as Muzak from a clock radio. It is not that the plethora of lackluster Pinot Grigio tastes bad per se, but at considerable expense, they are often about as flavorful as those pulpy jugs of lemon water at health spas. To be fair, examples of Pinot Grigio with more complexity and oomph do exist, but the majority remains bland and muted, the wine equivalent of norm-core fashion.

Let's consider my favorite alternatives, ones that retain Pinot Grigio's pro-file of lighter weight, little to no oak, and prominent acidity, but with more personality:

1 VERDEJO (VEHR-DAY-HO, A GRAPE VARIETY FROM SPAIN)
Accessible, always pleasing burst of lemon-lime; from Spain's north-central area of Rueda; can be subtly evocative of fennel and other green herbs; gives fellow Spaniard Albariño a run for its money in vivacious approachability; fru-gally priced.

2 ASSYRTIKO (AH-SEAR-TEE-KOE, A GRAPE VARIETY) AND OTHER WHITES FROM GREECE
Light- to medium-weight rejuvenators with an enduring crush on white, flaky fish; the palate-whetting Assyrtiko from the isle of Santorini is particularly lemony and minerally; Moschofilero (mo-sko-FEE-leh-ro) is clean, smooth, and subtly peachy; shorten it to "Mosko" to avoid stuttering.

3 CHABLIS (SHAH-BLEE, A REGION IN FRANCE)
The Hitchcock blonde: Chardonnay at its purest and most elegant; moderate heft with lemony brightness and green apple tang; trademark flinty minerality and rapier thrusts of crispness; can be lightly creamy, but never leaden or dead-eningly oaky; gets pricey, though fine entry-level versions abound; has nothing to do with the jug wine of the same name.

4 RIESLING (REESE-LING, A GRAPE VARIETY) FROM AUSTRALIA
Not what you would expect from an Aussie white: bone-dry, vital, with acidity as bright as sunlight glinting off the Sydney Opera House; lithe, sleek

frame; lemon-limey tang, sometimes with floral or peachy undertones; often overlooked and underpriced.

5 FIANO (FEE-AH-NOH, A GRAPE VARIETY FROM ITALY)
One of Italy's great whites; light- to medium-framed zingster in cahoots with flowers and almonds; sometimes finishes with a hint of nuts or ginger; mostly from southern Italy's Campania region; mid-range in price.

6 MUSCADET (MOOSE-CAH-DAY, A GRAPE VARIETY FROM FRANCE)
Classic oyster wine from France's Loire Valley; clean, exuding citrus and salt; can be too neutral for some; small-batch versions sometimes offer complexity and ageability; fully committed to shellfish platters and goat cheese; still miraculously underpriced.

7 FRIULANO (FREE-OH-LAHN-OH, A GRAPE VARIETY FROM ITALY)
Mellifluous secret password for middleweight revivification; minerally or almondlike edge; a pride of northwestern Italy; used to be called "Tocai Fruilano."

8 VINHO VERDE (VEEN-YO VEHR-DEH, A STYLE OF WINE FROM PORTUGAL)
Frisky Portuguese white so thrillingly inexpensive it restores faith in humanity; sometimes slightly fizzy; superlative picnic wine or "house white"; easy citrusy irrigation for flaming-hot food.

9 SAUVIGNON BLANC (SOE-VEEN-YOHN BLAHNK, FROM CHILE)
Flavorful zingers, often melon-y, and made in a softer, Californian style; occasionally more vivacious and grassy à la Sancerre; the second-most-planted grape in Chile; very reliable; Casablanca is the key region; sold for a song.

10 ARNEIS (AR-NAYZ, A GRAPE VARIETY FROM ITALY)
Likable peachy, floral white from northern Italy's Piemonte region; its name translates to "little rascal"; soul mates with seafood; unsung hero of spicy Szechuan fare.

ALSO CONSIDER

ALIGOTÉ (AH-LEE-GO-TAY, A GRAPE VARIETY FROM FRANCE)
The other white wine from Burgundy; citrusy and super dry; chalky, with rippling acidity that disenchants those who avoid pickles and olives; takes patience to source.

DRY SHERRY (A STYLE OF WINE FROM SPAIN)

Not an easygoing gulp for novices unaccustomed to its salty, nutty, almost oceanic bent; has devoted geek following among those who prize its appetite-stoking abilities; for dry, light styles, seek "Fino" and "Manzanilla"; invitingly priced; classic with almonds, olives, or oysters.

RIESLING FROM THE FINGER LAKES, NEW YORK

Cool-climate source for the best American Riesling; apples and flowers laced with energetic, lip-smacking acidity; sometimes a touch of sweetness, the level of which may be indicated on the back label; often gets lost in the shuffle of other regions, but worth a special look; modestly priced.

RIESLING FROM GERMANY

Motherland of Riesling; somm obsession, but difficult-to-decipher labels and hard-to-predict sweetness disheartens the uninitiated; enchanting swirl of flowers, stone fruits, and sometimes a whiff of gasoline; ranges from fully dry (often labeled "Trocken") to fully sweet; legendarily flexible with food.

SAVENNIÈRES (SAH-VEH-NYAIR, A REGION IN FRANCE)

Citrusy exhilarator of the vinoscenti; typically super-dry version of Chenin Blanc emanating from France's Loire Valley; tiny growing area; faint notes of honey, ginger, or beeswax; tart austerity can be off-putting to pure pleasure seekers; the rare white that often benefits from decanting and aging.

SANCERRE (SAHN-SAIR, A REGION IN FRANCE)

An explosion of energetic, crackly, flinty goodness; brightly citric and determinedly herbal; sometimes piercingly dry; prices have crept up as consumers know to order it for their acid-herbal fix; too much personality for some.

SAUVIGNON BLANC FROM CALIFORNIA

Savvie with a duller dagger; less acid-herbal aggression, more weight and overt fruit flavors; attractive middle ground for those seeking a compromise between racy and rich.

SAUVIGNON BLANC FROM NEW ZEALAND

Explosively love-it-or-leave-it nose of citrus, grass, and passion fruit; charged up like a Tesla, with fluorescently bright acidity; reliable quality across producers; bespoke fit for scallops and bivalves.

VERMENTINO (VEHR-MEN-TEEN-OH, A GRAPE VARIETY FROM ITALY)

Gentlest gateway beyond Pinot Grigio; most famously from the Italian island of Sardinia, but important in Liguria and Tuscany as well; racy acidity with delicate suggestions of flower and nectarines; minerals often emerge on the finish; stock it like soda in summer.

OLDMAN'S 10 BEST

Alternatives to Chardonnay

Let's get it out of the way: Chardonnay is not over, and fine versions still account for the largest proportion of the world's great white wines. Strangulatingly oaky versions celebrated a generation ago are out of style, and many winemakers have dialed back their use of oak contact accordingly, sometimes to the extent of employing no oak at all. The fact remains that many of us remain admirers of whites of fuller weight and intensity. If you are looking to diversify beyond Chardonnay, and avoid the higher markup we pay for its fame, here is where to start:

1 ALBARIÑO (AL-BAH-REEN-YO, A GRAPE VARIETY, FROM SPAIN)

Seafood-obsessed, citrusy Spaniard; medium-figured with vibrant acidity; occasional hints of peaches, ginger, or almonds; excellent value with some price creep as its profile rises; everybody seems to like it.

2 VIOGNIER (VEE-OH-NYAY, A GRAPE VARIETY, FROM FRANCE)

Voluptuously textured white with a tropical, exotic perfume; moderate to full weight, with the softness and texture of Chardonnay, but with little or no oak; most commonly from the West Coast or France's Rhône Valley; versions from Virginia are also surprisingly enticing; penchant for seafood and fruit-based preparations.

3 GODELLO (GO-DAY-OH, A GRAPE VARIETY, FROM SPAIN)

Sportily Jamaican-sounding name for a future Spanish star; rich but brightly crisp, floral, melon-y, or ginger-tinged; sometimes a creamy finish; light oak, if any; interesting, lesser-known alternative to Albariño; yearns for plates of tapas.

4 GRÜNER VELTLINER (GREWN-AIR FELT-LEAN-AIR, A GRAPE VARIETY, FROM AUSTRIA)

Austria's most famous wine; medium-bodied with hints of citrus, peach, and a trademark dusting of white pepper; famously veggie-friendly; some simple ones come in one-liter, pop-top bottles; no longer quite as obsessed over by somms.

5 TORRONTÉS (TORE-RAHN-TEZ, A GRAPE VARIETY, FROM ARGENTINA)

Argentina's increasingly popular medium-bodied white; dichotomous sweet-smelling, floral perfume, but dry taste; perilously easy to drink and a good deal.

6 GEWÜRZTRAMINER (GUH-VURTS-TRAH-MEE-NER, A GRAPE VARIETY, FROM ALSACE, FRANCE)

Alsatian standard with coppery color and signature litchi, spice, and rosewater perfume; medium to full body; soft, round, sometimes unctuous texture; glad-hands spicy food; big personality makes it as polarizing as cilantro or Kanye West; pronouncing it creates hushed, admiring silence.

7 RHÔNE-STYLE WHITES, FROM THE WEST COAST AND AUSTRALIA

Unique, pornographically slippery whites often featuring the Roussanne or Marsanne grape; traditionally from France's Rhône Valley; fine examples from California's Central Coast and Australia; raisins, pears, ginger, honeysuckle; not everyone's dish.

8 PINOT GRIS (PEE-NOH GREE, A GRAPE VARIETY, FROM ALSACE, FRANCE)

Soft, rich, and spicy with notes of honey; expressive nature rockets it to a different solar system from Italy's Pinot Grigio despite the two being the same grape; generally not quite as spicy as the Alsatian Gewürztraminer.

9 FALANGHINA (FAH-LAN-GHEE-NAH, A GRAPE VARIETY, FROM ITALY)

Unpretentious, mellow, medium-weight; sometimes shades richer with suggestions of tangerine or ginger; mostly from the southern Italian region of Campania; wallet savior in restaurants.

10 RIOJA (REE-OH-HAH, A REGION IN SPAIN) BLANCO (I.E., WHITE RIOJA)

Lesser-known white blend overshadowed by the region's famous reds; usually dominated by the Viura grape; modern versions are medium framed and zesty, while traditional styles can be oaky, rounder, and plusher, sometimes hinting at tropical fruits and smoke or coconut; mercifully inexpensive; fun to show people that Rioja has a white side.

ALSO CONSIDER

CHENIN BLANC (SHEN-IN BLAHNK, FROM SOUTH AFRICA)

South Africa's signature white sadly stalled out in the Other Whites section of wine stores; apples, pears, and cantaloupe fan out on the palate; sometimes a smidgen of honey or minerals; crisp, but not to the extent of Chenin Blanc

—versions from France; called "Steen" by nostalgic locals; magnanimously priced.

CHÂTEAUNEUF-DU-PAPE BLANC (SHAH-TOW NUF DEW PAHP BLAHNK, A STYLE OF WINE, FROM FRANCE)

Rare white from the southern Rhône's most exalted appellation for reds; exotically positioned with apple or tropical fruit aromas, often joined by macadamia-like nuttiness and stony acidity; starts pricey (in the $30s) and can rise to triple that or more.

DRY FURMINT (FUR-MINT, FROM HUNGARY)

Not the sour detective from the OJ trial, but a complex Hungarian with a distinctive nose of flowers, pear, and smoke; bristles with life and a creamy finish; same grape as the bewitching dessert wines of Tokaj; gaining minor celebrity in wine circles.

DRY SÉMILLON (SEH-MEE-YHON, A GRAPE VARIETY, FROM AUSTRALIA)

Schizo personality because of its zesty and grapefruit-y nature in youth, and its buttercup-yellow, soft, honey-fig lusciousness with age; beloved in Aussieland, where they pronounce it "SEM-eh-lon,"; takes searching mate.

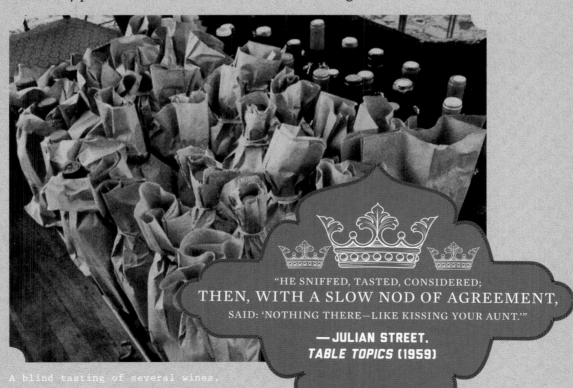

"HE SNIFFED, TASTED, CONSIDERED;
THEN, WITH A SLOW NOD OF AGREEMENT,
SAID: 'NOTHING THERE—LIKE KISSING YOUR AUNT.'"

—JULIAN STREET,
TABLE TOPICS (1959)

A blind tasting of several wines.

OLDMAN'S 10 BEST
Alternatives to Pinot Noir

If my desert island had electricity and a wine fridge with room for just one type, it would be crammed to the last inch with Pinot Noir. Where from? Doesn't matter. Give me the earthy, nuanced, lighter-style Pinots from its spiritual homeland of Burgundy, or the relatively delicate renditions from Oregon, New Zealand, northern Italy, or Germany. Or stock my fridge with the richer-style, sun-ripened Pinot from Sonoma's Russian River Valley or Santa Barbara's Santa Rita Hills.

Regardless of style, Pinot Noir is primed to deliver a silky swallow that is relatively light, low in tannin, and bursting with juicy red fruits like cherries and raspberries, often joined by suggestions of earth or wood smoke. Such a vibrant, sensual grape doesn't surrender its charms easily; its infamously temperamental nature makes the wine generally more expensive than many others. This is why it is so rewarding to know where else to look for Pinot-like airiness, acidity, and adaptability with food:

1 BEAUJOLAIS CRU (BOH-JOH-LAY, A REGION IN FRANCE) CREW
Lithe, gorgeous, floral reds still neglected by casual drinkers; raspberries and cranberries, with hints of violets, topsoil, or minerals; mouthwatering crispness; pairs with everything; startlingly inexpensive for the joy it engenders, though small-batch bottles fetch more; primary name on label is not "Beaujolais," but one of the "cru" villages, such as Morgon or Fleurie (see chart on page 40); every restaurant should be required to stock it.

2 BLAUFRÄNKISCH (BLAHW-FRANK-ISH, A GRAPE VARIETY, FROM AUSTRIA)
Death metal name for an eminently likable red from Austria; vibrant strawberry or cherry perfume, often with mineral accents and animated acidity; most are of medium build and well priced; leaves plenty of room for food.

3 CHINON (SHEE-NOWN), BOURGUEIL (BOOR-GOY), AND OTHER REDS, FROM THE LOIRE (FRANCE)
Bistro staple and trusted ally of value-minded somms and Francophiles; moderate weight with zesty red-berry flavors; violets, herbs, and perhaps a crank of pepper; from the Cabernet Franc grape, but other, more obscure Loire reds use Pinot Noir or Gamay; invigorating and versatile on Thanksgiving.

4 BIERZO (BEE-AIR-SO, A REGION IN SPAIN)
Supple enchantress from northwestern Spain that's gaining popularity; fresh, floral, moderate mouthfeel with red fruit, spice, and sometimes licorice; primary grape is Mencía; at its best gives Pinot Noir a run for its money, though sometimes finishes with pronounced but manageable bitterness.

5 CABERNET FRANC (CAB-ER-NAY FRAHN, FROM VARIOUS NEW WORLD REGIONS)
The other Cabernet; moderate weight with black cherry and tobacco leaf, sometimes a suggestion of cedar or earth; richer styles from California, Chile, and Argentina; leaner, if somewhat less consistent, versions from New York, Washington State, and Virginia; friendly to bank accounts.

6 NERELLO MASCALESE (NEH-REHL-LOH MAHS-KAH-LEH-ZEH, A GRAPE, FROM ITALY)
Mouthwateringly crisp, Pinot stand-in made in the shadow of Sicily's Mount Etna; grilled herbs, smoke, and minerality make you dream of the nearby volcano; craves red sauce dishes with garlic sliced *Goodfellas* thin.

7 RIOJA (REE-OH-HAH, A REGION IN SPAIN) CRIANZA (CREE-AHN-ZAH)
Everyday style of the classic Spanish blend dominated by the Tempranillo grape; slender body because Crianza level sees the least oak; cherries, plum, and earth, sometimes tinged with tobacco; dirt cheap because it lacks trendiness and complexity.

8 ZWEIGELT (TSVIE-GELT, A GRAPE VARIETY FROM AUSTRIA)
Not an Eastern European character actor but a lissome, bewitching red that prospers in cool regions; dried raspberry, savory herbs, and pepper converge on a feathery frame.

9 POULSARD, TROUSSEAU, AND OTHER REDS, FROM JURA FRANCE
Unusual, lesser-known, porcelain-boned slingshots of red berries and claylike minerality; sometimes a tinge of cinnamon or clove; starting to shed its obscurity, but still overlooked in favor of the Jura's more acclaimed funky whites; somm favorite and flexible with food.

10 ROSÉ (FROM EVERYWHERE)
Incorporates many features of a light red such as Pinot Noir; lighter weight, absence of bitter tannins, mile-wide versatility with food; encompasses everything from the lean, pale likes of Provençal rosé and fruity, savory Rioja Rosado to richer Mourvèdre-based Tavel and the cherry charms of Pinot Noir rosé from California; do not confine to summer; humanely priced.

ALSO CONSIDER

CHIANTI (KEE-AHN-TEE, A REGION IN ITALY)

Orange-tinted joke of yesteryear reinvented as a high-quality, Sangiovese-based red from Tuscany; like a savory, rosemary-scented, determinedly dry Pinot Noir that necessitates food; choose carefully; "Classico" indicates better quality, as does "Riserva," both of which are richer and more nuanced; tart cherry savoriness synergizes with black olives, tomatoes, and so much else.

FRAPPATO (FRAH-PAH-TOE, A GRAPE VARIETY FROM ITALY)

Floral red, as fun and sprightly as its pronunciation; generally light colored and svelte; from volcanic soils in Sicily; often blended with Nero d'Avola, but increasingly allowed to stand alone; destined for pizza.

GAMAY NOIR (A GRAPE VARIETY, FROM NORTH AMERICA)

A sprinkling of new-gen West Coast winemakers are having success with this grape, the same one used in Beaujolais; sour cherry, earth, with scant, if any, tannin; delicate, earthy examples also emerging from Canada's Niagara Peninsula.

LANGHE NEBBIOLO (LAHN-GUH NEH-B'YOH-LOW, A STYLE OF WINE FROM ITALY)

Less costly, dense, and tannic than Nebbiolo grape-based cousins Barolo and Barbaresco; less complex, too, with a medium body and cherry-raspberry and tobacco personality; sometimes a whiff of licorice, tar, and firm tannins; reveres risotto.

ROSSO DI MONTALCINO (ROW-SOH DEE MON-TALL-CHEE-NOH, A STYLE OF WINE FROM ITALY)

Sangiovese-powered kiss of black cherries, bitter herbs, and earth; ready young, unlike its richer, more tannic and costly sibling Brunello; tomato-based dishes call its name.

SCHIAVA (SKI-AH-VAH, A GRAPE VARIETY, FROM ALTO ADIGE, ITALY)

Lesser-known, bantamweight, crisp red from Italy's northeast; candied red fruits and crushed violets; cool it down like iced tea and drink it like a white.

VALPOLICELLA (VAL-PO-LEE-CHEL-LAH, A REGION IN ITALY)

As fashionable as bell-bottoms, but good versions charm; fresh, light to medium whoosh of cherries and raspberries; not wallet inflaming; from lesser-known grapes; versions labeled "Ripasso" (i.e., repassed through partially dried grapes) are darker and richer; don't hide the salumi.

VINO NOBILE DI MONTEPULCIANO (NOH-BEE-LAY DEE MAWN-TEH-POOL-CHA-NOH, A STYLE OF WINE, FROM ITALY)
Along with Brunello and Chianti, one of the three great Sangiovese-based wines of Tuscany; black cherry and plum, joined by leather and coffee; not cheap, but less draining than Brunello.

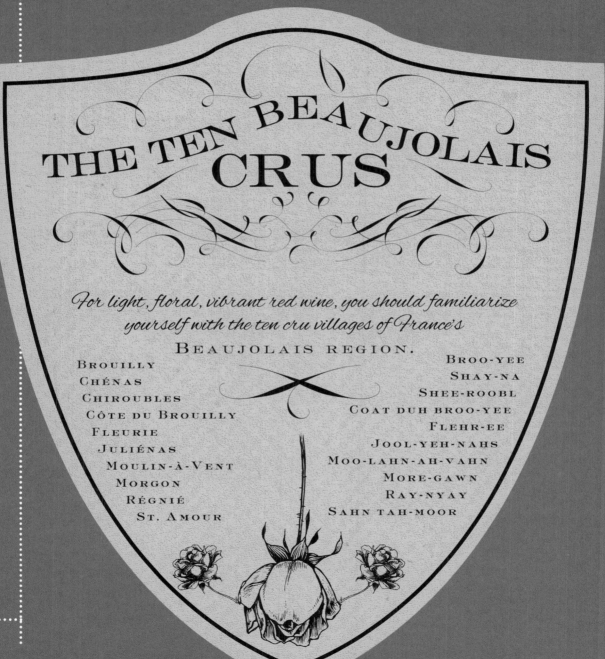

THE TEN BEAUJOLAIS CRUS

For light, floral, vibrant red wine, you should familiarize yourself with the ten cru villages of France's

BEAUJOLAIS REGION.

BROUILLY	BROO-YEE
CHÉNAS	SHAY-NA
CHIROUBLES	SHEE-ROOBL
CÔTE DU BROUILLY	COAT DU BROO-YEE
FLEURIE	FLEHR-EE
JULIÉNAS	JOOL-YEH-NAHS
MOULIN-À-VENT	MOO-LAHN-AH-VAHN
MORGON	MORE-GAWN
RÉGNIÉ	RAY-NYAY
ST. AMOUR	SAHN TAH-MOOR

"Rosé season *lasts twelve months per year*"

—Mark

OLDMAN'S 10 BEST
Alternatives to Cabernet Sauvignon and Merlot

Nothing will dethrone King Cabernet's supremacy for full-bodied, robust red wine. It comprises many of world's most exalted reds, both as a stand-alone grape in places such California and Australia and in blends such as the majority of red Bordeaux and certain so-called super Tuscans from Italy. Princely Merlot, with a profile similar to Cabernet's, often with less heft and tannin, is also here to stay, no matter how much the motion picture *Sideways* deflated its mojo. Despite an overabundance of bland commercial versions, Merlot is another global great, powering polished, complex reds from Italy, California, and Bordeaux's Right Bank.

With these marquee wine types selling at a premium, let's consider these tempting alternatives:

1 REDS FROM PORTUGAL
Deserves to be wine's next big thing, but probably won't because of the foreign names and unfamiliar indigenous grapes (none of which you need to know about); dried currant and roasted plum with trademark slatey minerality; a screaming buy for the quality; Douro is the primary region, but look to Dao and Alentejo for pulse-racing values.

2 SYRAH FROM WASHINGTON STATE
Tapenade-dark, velvety wines of polish and expressiveness; blackcurrants braided with black pepper, smoke, or perhaps a dusting of clove; often a better value than the equivalent from Napa and often slightly less dense; reliable quality makes it a triumph of American winemaking; deals abound as do costly bottles.

3 MALBEC (A GRAPE VARIETY, FROM ARGENTINA)
Luscious Argentine cheek plumper brimming with blueberry and other dark berries; often shows a bittersweet Godiva dimension; industry success story for achieving prime-time status; the beef (especially gaucho steak) sizzles here.

4 PRIMITIVO (PREE-ME-TEE-VO, A GRAPE, ITALY) AND OTHER REDS, FROM PUGLIA
Unpretentious, giving wines from Italy's sunny south; hearty, deep black fruits, with rustic renditions evoking raisins or prunes; the same grape as America's Zinfandel; Puglia's Salice Salentino from the Negromaro grape has

a similar personality; reliable low-cost seduction on the coldest winter night; desperately seeking eggplant parmigiana.

5 REDS FROM LANGUEDOC-ROUSSILLON (LAHN-GUH-DOC ROO-SEE-YOHN, FRANCE)
Prolific region of southern France often overlooked by American consumers; surge of ripe, dark berries with mineral, mocha, or lightly peppery accents; in the mix are often Rhône-style grapes such as Syrah and Grenache; know the subregions of Corbières, Faugères, and Minervois; searching for its next saucisson sandwich.

6 AGLIANICO (AH-LEE-AH-NEH-KO, A GRAPE VARIETY, FROM ITALY)
Rich, savory black-fruited swagger of sour cherry, leather, black olive, or smoke; top wine of relatively humble southern Italy; can be too tannic for some; not insultingly pricey; positioned for porterhouse and rib eye.

7 MONASTRELL (MOHN-AH-STREHL, A GRAPE VARIETY, FROM SPAIN)
Cut-price Spanish reds from the grape known as Mourvèdre (moor-ved) outside Spain; full-throttled, plush spread of black cherry and plum; sometimes a smoky or gamy edge; recessionary pricing; look for the regions of Jumilla (who-MEE-ah), Yecla, and Alicante.

8 GSM BLENDS AND REDS, FROM PASO ROBLES, CALIFORNIA
Bold, flamboyant, heady power chords from this sun-brightened patch of California's Central Coast, halfway between San Francisco and Los Angeles; often Rhône-style blends of Grenache, Syrah, and Mourvèdre; Zinfandel also popular in Paso; plush, ripe, peppery swoosh of blackberries and plums; first in line at the barbecue.

9 ZINFANDEL, FROM CALIFORNIA
Robust, uniquely Californian bicep flex of black fruits; many flavor-stoking old-vine vineyards; more intensely fruity than its counterpart in Italy, the aforementioned Primitivo; cozies up to anything blackened, grilled, or kebabified.

10 BARBERA (BAR-BEAR-AH, A GRAPE, FROM ITALY)
Popular blackberry deliverer of nightly joy from Italy's Piedmont region and the Asti or Alba sub-zones therein; currants and plums, with buzzing acidity; reliably smooth with some exceptions; almost always a good deal; homes in on pizza and Sunday gravy with the efficacy of an Air Force drone.

ALSO CONSIDER

CARMÉNÈRE (CAR-MEN-YARE, A GRAPE VARIETY, FROM CHILE)

Deeply hued, rich red flourishing in Chile; plum, cherry, sometimes tobacco leaf; palate-carpeting texture; memorize the name for key value at steak houses.

CÔTES DU RHÔNE (A REGION IN FRANCE)

Long-adored wintertime antivenom; meaty, savory red from the southern Rhône Valley; round, relatively low acidity but sometimes an edgy rusticity; medium to full scale; low cost inspires double takes.

DOLCETTO (DOL-CHET-OH, A GRAPE VARIETY, FROM ITALY)

Medium-bodied, plummy zinger from Italy's Piemonte region; rarely oaky; its translation, "little sweet one," belies its often pleasant bitterness; excellent everyday quaff and priced for Tuesday-night meatballs.

GIGONDAS AND VACQUEYRAS (JHEE-GOHN-DAS AND VAH-KAY-RAHSS, REGIONS IN FRANCE)

Dark-berry savoriness and earth from the southern Rhône; relatively affordable alternative to famous Châteauneuf-du-Pape; perfect with lusty food like stews and roasts.

LAGREIN (LAH-GRINE, A GRAPE VARIETY, FROM ITALY)

Middleweight red from Italy's northeasterly Alto Adige region; black plum with notes of herbs or pepper; can be surprisingly tannic; denser versions occasionally surface; gently priced but not the easiest to find.

PETITE SIRAH (PEH-TEET SEE-RAH, A GRAPE VARIETY, FROM CALIFORNIA)

Massive, dark, Californian hulkster; a heady eruption of blackberries, black tea, and black pepper; often confused with Syrah, a different grape with a similar personality.

REDS FROM BANDOL, FRANCE

Not famous like the rosé of this Provençal region, but it quietly gets it done with dark, rich, and ferrous-scented gems; possible echoes of anise, juniper, or bay leaf; a blend of several grapes, most prominently Mourvèdre; not abundant in the U.S., but a French wine specialist can steer you there; demands thick slices of country charcuterie.

RIOJA RESERVA AND GRAN RESERVA (A REGION IN SPAIN)

Gloriously untrendy, medium- to full-figured fandangos of black fruits, smoke, and tilled-soil earthiness; sometimes a hint of leather or espresso; sweet-spot prices sprinkled with a few deluxe offerings; clear your throat on the final syllable of Rioja.

SHIRAZ (SHE-RAHZ, A GRAPE VARIETY, FROM AUSTRALIA)

Aussie explosion of plush, expressive black fruits, sweet spice, and licorice; often woozily high alcohol, but some vintners now reining that in; supermarket success of Yellowtail disguises its capability of making exquisitely complex editions; put it to work with lamb chops.

ST.-JOSEPH (SAHN JHO-SEF, A REGION IN FRANCE)

Medium- to full-framed, cherry-violet, mineral-laced stand-ins for the more expensive and complex wines of northern Rhône, such as Hermitage and Côte Rôtie; not abundant on these shores; magical with stews and roasts.

SYRAH (SEAR-AH, A GRAPE VARIETY, FROM CALIFORNIA)

Big, brash, and intense with telltale notes of black pepper, black olive, and leather; not dainty, and its supporters love it that way; same grape as Shiraz from Australia.

OLDMAN'S 10 BEST
Special Occasion Wines

If a wine's cost is not always proportional to its deliciousness, the question remains as to whether special occasion wine is worth the price. Look at it this this way: When you occasionally overspend for a bottle, you are buying more than just the taste of a wine. You are investing in a memory, from the anticipation and acquisition of the bottle to its consumption and perhaps a late-night spooning with the empty bottle. I like to tell people that special occasion wine is also a socially acceptable way of flipping off the banalities and indignities of life, an indulgence that is less expensive and more social than fine art, collectable cars, or an addiction to Amazon Prime. My favorite special occasion wine types are as follows:

BUBBLY AND WHITE

1 CHAMPAGNE (FRANCE)
F. Scott Fitzgerald wasn't wrong when he wrote, "Too much of anything is bad, but too much Champagne is just right." Winston Churchill would have agreed, as he reportedly spent more than $100,000 a year on his bubbly habit. You'll never go wrong if you remember my catchphrase "Always Champagne": big brand or indie; by itself or with food; nonvintage or expensive prestige cuvée; with elevated dishes or a can of Pringles; shimmeringly fresh or honeyedly mature. Just make it cold and make it count.

2 WHITE BURGUNDY (FRANCE)
Chardonnay at its most complex; generous but not heavy; fruity without being aggressively so; oaky, with shadings of vanilla or crème brûlée, but not sweet; finishes with minerality; know the famous villages of Meursault, Puligny-Montrachet, and Chassagne-Montrachet; dial "L" for lobster as often as possible.

3 CONDRIEU (COHN-DREE-UH, A REGION IN FRANCE)
The Viognier grape from the northern Rhône Valley; medium to full bodied and bone-dry; a buxom offering of tropical fruits, but with European restraint; wallet draining, rare, and worth considering an indecent proposal for.

4 CHARDONNAY (CALIFORNIA)

A Creamsicle with euphoric powers; at its best, a blast of nectarine, pine-apple, and butterscotch, balanced by plenty of vibrant acidity; not as lusted for in the media as it once was, but for many of us it remains the liquid embodiment of Coleridge's "Kubla Khan": "he on honey-dew hath fed / And drunk the milk of Paradise."

5 RIESLING (AUSTRIA)

Achtung! Brace yourself for Riesling that is rich, always dry, with a gleaming stream of apples, pears, and white pepper; scours your senses with a gloriously stony minerality; unlike the Rieslings of Germany, labels are straightforward, save for a sprinkling of Viennese-chic umlauts; prices start in the $30s and can be triple that.

RED

1 RED BURGUNDY

The slayer, the most nuanced, beguiling, romantic and expensive wine in the world; France's Burgundy region is also the world template for Pinot Noir; inconsistency bestows it with a feline elusiveness that makes aficionados anxious and poor and long for more; start with Volnay, a relatively reliable and accessible village; graduate to the grand cru vineyard Musigny, but not before mortgaging the house.

2 CABERNET SAUVIGNON (CALIFORNIA)

The ripe upstart: a lush, generous blackcurrant-y avatar of Californian sunlight; mint or juniper can emerge from the glass; texture is rich but typically smooth and polished; many connoisseurs' first serious love and one that never fades; like a thieving supermodel, it is expensive but worth the cost.

3 RED BORDEAUX (FRANCE)

Iconic, aristocratic blends usually dominated by Cabernet Sauvignon or Merlot; medium to full weight, often with prominent tannins when young; at its best, it shows profound complexity, with blackcurrant, tobacco, minerals, and often the signature scent of pencil lead; lamb is a soul mate; top chateaux have become dispiritingly costly.

4 BAROLO (ITALY)

Italy's regal, uncompromising expression of the Nebbiolo grape; Piemonte-based blockbuster that needs years of age to lose its sadistic sheath of tannins and acidity; fine, mature versions can be astonishingly unique in nose and taste; signature scent is tar and roses, but leather and menthol often rise to the fore; king's ransom in cost, but not as frightful as Burgundy and Bordeaux; almost a necessity to get food on the scene—ideally, rich fare like pasta saturated with butter and white truffles.

5 CHÂTEAUNEUF-DU-PAPE (SHAH-TOW-NUF DEW PAHP, A REGION IN FRANCE)

Southern Rhône Valley's most celebrated red; most are a blend dominated by the Grenache grape; pricey and nuanced, with roasted berry and bacon-y, savory goodness; bottles have embossed seals, which make them an extra-special gift; prays to the goddess of cassoulet.

ALSO CONSIDER

AMARONE (AM-AH-ROE-NEH, A TYPE OF WINE)

A powerful, swaggering capo; heady from dehydrated grapes grown in the Valpolicella district of Italy's Veneto region; bold, extravagantly priced, high-octane taste that often requires ten or more years to mellow; sometimes has an intriguing cocoa-and-minerals quality; deserves to be drunk in a jewel-encrusted chalice.

BRUNELLO DI MONTALCINO (BREW-NEL-LO DEE MON-TAHL-CHEE-NO, A STYLE OF WINE FROM ITALY)

The Titan of Tuscany; zenith of prestige and power drawn from the Sangiovese grape; cherry and plum; sometimes a distinct herbal or licorice edge; astringent in youth, so give it some years; aftertaste can evoke leather or coffee; bull's-eye pick with Florentine steak.

HERMITAGE (AIR-ME-TAHJ, A REGION IN FRANCE)

Northern Rhône's mythical red; complex, Syrah-based power player; blackberry, crushed rock, olive, pepper, sometimes bacon or game or beef teriyaki; needs years to mellow; at home with hearty winter fare and peppery sauces.

RIBERA DEL DUERO (REE-BEAR-AH DELL DWAIR-OH, A REGION IN SPAIN)

Rich and smoky, with prominent tannins courtesy of the Tempranillo grape; ambitious bottles show complexity and sometimes considerable tannin; includes Spain's top wine, Vega Sicilia.

SUPER TUSCANS (A STYLE OF WINE FROM ITALY)

Brash, complex, blackberry-scented reds from Tuscany; often notes of savory spice or tar; gained fame in the 1970s by using growing areas and nonlocal grapes (e.g., Cabernet Sauvignon, Merlot, etc.) originally unsanctioned by Italian wine authorities; fanciful names that often end in -aia, such as the legendary Saississicaia, Ornellaia, and Solaia.

OLDMAN'S 10 BEST
Alternatives to Big-Brand Champagne

Life would be a dimmer, grimmer affair without the marquee names of Champagne. These are the brands that embody the lustrous and convivial spirit of wine itself. From entry-level Louis Roederer Brut Premier to artist edition versions of Dom Pérignon, this is where pinpoint bubbles, baked-bread aromas, and creamy, nuanced flavors meld into one glorious whole. If I set the rules, every citizen would be required to keep a bottle on the refrigerator shelf, poised and ready, like a reverse panic button for life's little victories. With its tony packaging, omnipresent marketing, and high tariffs, however, big name Champagne is as much of a luxury purchase as anything you'd find in downtown Dubai. Luckily for us, a galaxy of attractive alternatives exist beyond Champagne's yellow labels and art nouveau anemones. These are the best:

1 GROWER CHAMPAGNE
The indie, mom-and-pop Champagne makers who grow their own grapes rather than buy them from outside growers; high quality and usually less costly than the klieg-light names; more likely to express the terroir of one specific vineyard site, while the big houses blend grapes of many vineyards; limited production makes it difficult to consistently find the same producers; typically signaled by an "RM" in the microscopically sized serial number on the label (larger, négociant-manipulant producers are represented by a tiny "NM"); call it "farmer fizz"; favorites include Agrapart, Bara, Bérêche, Billiot, Gimonnet, Egly-Ouriet, Ledru, Lemandier-Bernier, Selosse, Tarlant, and Vilmart.

2 AMERICAN SPARKLING WINE
Like a classically trained rock star, American sparkling wine combines traditional technique with Yankee verve; more likely to show ripe fruit than toasty or minerally aromas; rosé versions cotton to almost any item on a menu, including spice; California and Oregon are mainstay sources; excitingly undervalued.

3 CAVA (SPAIN)
Winsome, traditionally made Spanish sparkler; lighter and less complex than Champagne; from lesser-known Spanish grapes such as Xarello (zuh-REL-oh); wonderfully underpriced; the world glows brighter with its universal availability.

4 PROSECCO (ITALY)

Pavlovian trigger for joy, not unlike the words "pizza," "sex," or "yes"; lightly sparkling, with juicy apple and melon character; lack of expense partially attributable to tank method of deriving bubbles; typically dry taste can sometimes display a tinge of sweetness; killjoy sommeliers dismiss it as too simple, while the rest of us happily pop our "Prozac-co"; be wary of bland commercial versions.

5 CRÉMANT (CRAY-MAWN, FRANCE)

Name for French sparkling wine made outside of the northeasterly Champagne region; tends to be insistently crisp and often lighter than Champagne; made in regions all over France, with Crémant d'Alsace the most common; also watch for Crémant de Loire, Crémant de Bourgogne, and Crémant de Limoux.

6 DRY LAMBRUSCO (A GRAPE VARIETY FROM ITALY)

Savory sparkling red from Italy not to be confused with semisweet commercial Lambrusco; a lunar-dark, cherry-smoky little engine that can; light to medium weight with vitalizing acidity; possible whiff of spice or licorice; fantastically versatile with food, from pizza to the entirety of a Thanksgiving feast to any fatty compound you throw at it; tracking down small, artisanal producers requires effort.

7 FRANCIACORTA (FRAN-CHA-CORE-TAH, A REGION IN ITALY)

Fine, traditionally made from Italy's Lombardy region; stylistically a far cry from Prosecco's summery fun; capable of greatness but sometimes lacks Champagne's concentration and complexity; not priced for daily use.

8 SPARKLING SHIRAZ (A TYPE OF WINE, FROM AUSTRALIA)

Simple, dark bubbly built for merriment; masters Asian food with fruity, effervescent efficiency; Aussies, bless 'em, will sometimes drink it with breakfast; little-known nickname is "spurgle," a mash-up of "sparkling" and "Burgundy."

9 TXAKOLI (CHOC-OH-LEE, SPAIN)

Spanish Basque sea spray in a bottle; lightly fizzy with a salty, sea-foamy taste; casual, low in alcohol, and tumbler ready; nutty and briny flavor can disconcert those with Champagne expectations; chug it from a porron (chapter 112).

10 TASMANIAN SPARKLING WINE (A TYPE OF WINE, FROM AUSTRALIA)

Not punch lines but crisp, generously flavorful sparklers from Oz's cool-climate island; not many get to these shores, but worth the effort to secure; call it a "Tassie" sparkler for insider cred.

ALSO CONSIDER

BRITISH SPARKLING WINE

Growing category of traditionally made sparkling wine from the advanta-geously chalky soils of southern England; has benefited from region's warming climate; recent purchase of a UK vineyard by French Champagne house Tait-tinger's is a major vote of confidence; ask for "Brit fizz"; finding bottles might require a dragnet; names to know include Chapel Down, Coats & Seely, Gus-bourne, Herbert Hall, and Ridgeview.

PÉTILLANT-NATUREL (A STYLE OF WINE, FROM LOIRE, FRANCE, AND EVERYWHERE)

Playful style of bubbly; less expensive and complex than Champagne; bubbles come from bottling the wine before primary fermentation is finished (unlike Champagne, which undergoes a labor-intensive second fermentation); très hip because of its irresistible nickname "Pét-Nat" and emphasis on natural winemaking techniques; often cloudy, lightly bubbly (though carbonation can vary), and closed with a beerlike crown cap; not appreciated by all palates because sometimes sour or cider-y.

MAKE THEM COUGH UP
THE BUBBLES

If you are fortunate enough to be flying business class, your flight attendant will of course offer you white or red. The trick, I've discovered, is to know to ask for bubbly, which is a choice that is for some reason not well marketed on airplanes, especially on domestic routes. In fact, when I ask for it, the bubbly is often not on the cart at all, and the attendant has to call to her colleague to fish the bottle out of a drawer in the galley. (Sometimes they do so with palpable disappointment, as if you have co-opted their mid-flight refreshment.) No matter, you should ask for the sparkler, because it tends to be of equal or higher quality than the still wine choices, it goes with virtually every dish, and it won't weigh you down like a heavier wine.

OLDMAN'S 10 BEST
Dessert Wines

You owe it to yourself—in fact, I'll posit that you will lead a happier life—if you force yourself to start liking dessert wine. Too many of us avoid it because we misperceive it as too sweet and leaden. The reality is that styles abound that manage to stay vibrant while spiriting you into the night on a nectarous high. These are the best:

1 MOSCATO D'ASTI (ITALY)

A playful springtime kiss; charmingly light and crisp and delicately sweet; semi-sparkling, low in alcohol; factoring in its modest price, probably the best liquid meal ender in existence; a far cry from the cloyingly sweet, commericial Moscatos jostling for your attention.

2 SAUTERNES (SAW-TAIRN, A REGION IN FRANCE)

Rich, golden, ethereal elixir from Bordeaux; apricots, baked apple, honey; vigorous crispness counterbalances its sweetness; so special that I sneaked a taste of it at a hospital moments before three hours of spinal surgery to fix a pinched nerve; ageable, expensive, and worth every penny.

3 VINTAGE PORT (PORTUGAL)

Good bottles are the liquid essences of jet-set, high-grade fumes of Italian leather and brown sugar, like a deep dive into Jackie O's purse; the granddaddy of fortified wine; relatively costly, but a buying opportunity because overlooked on these shores; ageable for decades.

4 ICE WINE (CANADA AND GERMANY)

Intensely concentrated ambrosial whisk of tropical fruit undergirded by crisp acidity; Canada's vinous pride and joy; from grapes (especially Riesling or Vidal) left to freeze on the vine long after harvest; German counterpart is called "Eiswein," but is frustratingly rare; requires financial sacrifice.

5 TAWNY PORT (PORTUGAL)

Relatively affordable and lighter style of Port; ruby-brick colored; redolent of walnuts and toffee with a smidgen of orange peel or brown sugar; already aged for you, from ten to forty years; decadent with salty cheese or peanut brittle.

6 TOKAJI ASZÚ (TOH-KAY AH-SOO, A TYPE OF WINE, FROM HUNGARY)
Golden pleasure potion, similar in character to Sauternes; from Furmint and other local grapes; rated "D" for delectable; gives you the opportunity to purse your lips like a KGB agent and say the word "puttonyos" (poo-tun-yosh, a measure of the Tokaji's sweetness level).

7 VIN SANTO (A TYPE OF WINE, FROM ITALY)
Amber, nutty, datelike wine from grapes dried on straw mats; use biscotti as edible swizzle sticks (chapter 33).

8 VINTAGE MADEIRA (MUH-DEAR-UH, A REGION IN PORTUGAL)
Exotic-tasting fortified wine with telltale essences of caramel and nuts; hasn't been chic since the founding fathers dipped their fountain pens; from the eponymous Portuguese island in the middle of the Atlantic Ocean; ranges from dry to semidry to sweet; the most affordable way to drink very old wine, as it is often already aged for decades before release; lasts forever when opened, so there are multiple opportunities to enjoy the same bottle.

9 BANYULS (BAHN-YOOL, A REGION, FRANCE)
Lesser-known Grenache-based fortified wine from France's Languedoc-Roussillon region; a unique taste of dark fruit with hints of chocolate and orange peel; classic companion of dark chocolate; low profile can make it a compelling value.

10 BRACHETTO D'ACQUI (BRA-KAY-TOH DAH-KWEE, ITALY)
Charms like a heart-shaped pendant; from northern Italy; candied raspberry and cherry, joined by rose petals; lightly bubbly and delicately sweet, though some versions are a shade sweeter; not a negative bone in its body and more effective than roses on Valentine's Day.

OLDMAN'S 10 BEST
Obscure Wines

Despite the contentions of certain fanatics, obscure wines are not necessarily preferable to the better-known types. Their scarcity can make them frustrating to source and even harder to find again, although the Internet and specialist merchants improve the odds. More crucially, the appeal of esoteric wines is not always in their taste; sometimes, they generate desire by the mere fact that they play hard to get, while their taste is middling or even disorientating.

Disclaimers aside, novel grapes and regions that actually make delicious wine can be dazzlingly revelatory and economical. If you agree with Ernest Hemingway's recommendation of "life intoxicated by the romance of the unusual," then the following novel wine types will send you off buzzed with the thrill of discovery (in alphabetical order):

AGIORGITIKO (AH-YOR-YEE-TE-KO, A GRAPE VARIETY, GREECE)

Dark Greek red redolent of spicy blackberry and plum, sometimes with a smoky dimension; medium bodied, but occasionally plumper; you'll earn a vinous black belt comes by pronouncing it correctly.

FREISA (FRAY-ZUH, A GRAPE VARIETY, ITALY)

Light-colored, sometimes fizzy, medium-bodied red that resonates with wild strawberry; from Italy's Piemonte region and often from the Langhe region therein; has a crush on semi-hard cheese and house-cured meats.

GRIGNOLINO (GREE-NYOH-LEE-NOH, A GRAPE VARIETY, ITALY)

Simple but joyous feathery red quaff; often juicily acidic and lightly bitter on the finish; from Italy's Piemonte region, but California's Cab-famous Heitz Cellars has long made a rosé from it; priced to move; cools down spicy food.

KERNER (A GRAPE VARIETY, ITALY AND GERMANY)

Vaguely militaristic sounding white primarily from Italy's Alto-Adige region; fresh and floral, like a grapefruit-y Riesling; possible notes of peach or orange peel; mineral-laced finish; high quality, complex, and priced like it.

PICPOUL DE PINET (PICK-POOL DE PIN-AYE, FRANCE)

Not Run DMC lyrics or an Austin Powers nemesis but a fantastic oyster-loving oyster-loving white from France's southerly Languedoc-Roussillon; delicate, simple, and lemony; comes in tall, slim, green bottles; priced for the pauper in all of us.

PICOLIT (PEEK-OH-LEET, A GRAPE, ITALY)

Luscious dessert wine prized in its native Friuli Venezia Giulia region of northeast Italy; near-narcotic burst of apricots, honey, white flowers; my favorite gift for connoisseurs who think they've tasted it all; expensive and locating it may necessitate a K-9 unit.

REDS FROM VALLE D'AOSTA (VAHL-LAY DAY-OH-STAH, A REGION IN ITALY)

Edgily crisp, floral, airy reds from a tiny region tucked in the far northwestern corner of Italy, hard by France and Switzerland; often comprised of Gamay or intriguing local grapes.

RIBEIRA SACRA (REE-BEAR-AH SACK-RAH, A REGION IN SPAIN)

A rediscovered district of northwestern Spain making svelte, intriguing, juicy reds; from the Mencía grape, which also appears in the better-known wines of Bierzo; so far in short supply but could expand its presence.

RIBOLLA GIALLA (REE-BOHL-LAH JAHL-LAH, GRAPE A FROM ITALY)

Respected, indigenous grape from northeastern Italy's Friuli-Venezia Giulia, as well as Slovenia and a few from the United States; golden hued, medium bodied, with apple and lemony character but can shade to apricot-y with a round mouthfeel; the grape used in some of the most famous "orange wines" (i.e., white wines fermented on their skins like a red, such as Gravner's Ribolla Gialla).

ZIERFANDLER (ZEER-FAND-LUH, A GRAPE FROM AUSTRIA)

Not a Ben Stiller flick but a rare, indigenous grape that makes a charming, middleweight white; whiffs of yellow pear, apricot, or other tropical fruit; sometimes a buttery finish; microscopic bottle runs necessitate a thorough search.

ALSO CONSIDER

CHAMPAGNE USING FORGOTTEN GRAPES

Though most Champagne is made from Chardonnay and/or Pinot Noir, with sometimes a bit of Pinot Meunier blended in, some smaller Champagne producers push the boundaries by making surprisingly delicious all–Pinot

Meunier bottlings. These include Egly-Ouriet, Loriot, Laherte, Jérôme, and Prévost. Even more rare are the brave Champagne houses that make use of the other four ancient grapes that even dedicated bubbleheads don't know are allowed in Champagne: Arbanne, Petit Meslier, Pinot Gris, and Pinot Blanc. Houses embracing ancient grapes include Agrapart, Aspasie, Bérèche, Laherte, and Tarlant. If you can find them, you are in for a Champagne experience like no other.

UNCONVENTIONAL CALIFORNIAN WINES

A new generation of Cali winemakers is experimenting with lesser-known grapes such as Mouvèdre, Sémillon, and Trousseau, as well as nontraditional winemaking techniques. The fruits of these efforts are sometimes successful, sometimes not, but are rarely boring. Produced in small lots and thus difficult to find, these wines tend to be made in a more European, moderate-alcohol style than the hyper-ripe Californian style made famous a generation ago. These so-called new Californian wines encompass a wide array of wineries, including A Tribute to Grace, RPM, Dirty Rowdy, Lieu Dit, Rhys, and Soliste.

MORE ON WINE TYPES

NO. 0004

Mise en Bouteille au Domaine

13% ALC. BY VOL   PRODUCT OF NEW YORK   750 ML

16 HIGH-ALCOHOL WINES ARE NOT YOUR ENEMY

It seems innocent enough: Most wines range between 10 and 16 percent alcohol, the variance depending on the type of grape, vineyard location, winemaker preference, and, critically, on how ripe a wine's grapes are at harvest. The more sugar in the grapes, the more alcohol you have in the finished wine. So it follows that warmer-climate grapes that are allowed to get fully ripe tend to make wine at the upper end of the alcohol scale. Higher-alcohol wines also tend to have more body—think of the lean 12.8 percent Bourgogne rouge versus a mouth-filling 14.5 percent Californian Pinot Noir.

It is wine's equivalent of the Bud Light "tastes great, less filling" divide: Two vociferous, occasionally sneering camps have coalesced around what they think is the correct side of the alcohol debate. One says that wine should be rich and full throttle, conforming to über-critic Robert Parker's famous penchant for overripe "fruit bombs." On the other side are alcohol agonizers who say such high-octane "fruit bombs" are ungainly, lack nuance, and do not do justice to a grape type's natural expression. They contend, for example, that Californian Pinot Noir should not be allowed to get so lush and rich—that it should better approximate the leaner style we see in Pinot Noir from its homeland of Burgundy, France.

Here's the good news that neither side will tell you: There is no need to take sides. I tend to favor lower-alcohol wines because they are lighter, easy to drink, and tend to pair better with food. That lean, edgy Sancerre Rouge will be a better complement with food than the ultraripe Cabernet Sauvignon whose flavors can dominate dishes of delicate weight. But sometimes I hanker for a big, rich, potent red the way I'll sometimes forgo the chicken paillard for a creamy potpie. Those who would scoff at such wine for being less complex or refined fail to appreciate how much pleasure this style brings to so many people. And higher-alcohol content does not always have to burn like Bourbon if the wine has enough fruit flavor to balance the ample alcohol. I recently had a Zinfandel with 16.2 percent alcohol that was balanced by so much luscious pomegranate-y fruit that is was as pleasurable as a velvety pillowcase. And it was also a wine of great nuance and complexity. Nothing was more delightful to sip on a brisk autumn night.

Let the self-righteous bicker with one another about which style the world should prefer. You will have more opportunities for joy if you are "omnivinous" like me and find opportunities to enjoy both.

17 BLENDED WINES ARE NOT INFERIOR

When it comes to things we ingest, people seem to have an innate distrust of blends, as if they are a way to hide imperfect ingredients or to add filler. Perhaps it stems back to a fear of too much cake in the crab cake or dog in the hot dog, the latter being particularly relevant in certain shadowy corners of East Asia.

This concern extends to wine, with my students often mistakenly assuming that wine blended from more than one grape is not as good as so-called varietal wine—that is, wine primarily from one particular grape variety such as Riesling or Zinfandel. Most countries have laws that regulate the minimum percentage of a certain grape needed for the bottle to be labeled with that grape type; US law, for example, requires a wine labeled "Chardonnay" to contain at least 75 percent of the Chardonnay grape. What this means is that many of the wines we assume to be purely from one grape are actually themselves a blend.

Reputable wineries, however, are not exactly using the viticultural equivalent of Hamburger Helper to fill out the rest of their wine. Au contraire: good vintners often perform a bit of blending to add an extra dimension to their wine, such as using some soft Merlot to tone down the tannic astringency of Cabernet Sauvignon or mixing a small proportion of the Viognier with sturdy red Syrah to bestow it with more aromatic complexity.

If this fails to convince you that blends are not necessarily the wine equivalent of potluck, know that some of the world's most prestigious wines are unapologetic blends of different grape types. Champagne, for example, contains up to three different types of grapes sanctioned by the French government, and red Bordeaux mixes together up to five grape varieties. Napa Valley's Joseph Phelps's celebrated Insignia is a blend, as are other so-called meritage (rhymes with "heritage") Bordeaux-style blends, such as the blue-chip Dominus and Quintessa. Not all esteemed Californian wineries feel the need to follow Old World recipes: innovators such as Sean Thackery have created highly successful blends that include such unlikely bedfellows as Pinot Noir and Sangiovese.

A LABEL'S ALCOHOL PERCENTAGE MAY NOT BE ACCURATE

WITH SO MUCH DEBATE THESE DAYS OVER DESIRABLE ALCOHOL LEVELS IN WINE, IT IS SURPRISING THAT THE US GOVERNMENT ALLOWS WINEMAKERS AN ERROR RATE OF UP TO 1.5 PERCENT ON WINES UNDER 14 PERCENT ALCOHOL AND A VARIANCE OF 1 PERCENT FOR WINES OVER 14 PERCENT. WHILE THIS MAY NOT SOUND LIKE A LOT, IT ACTUALLY IS. IT MEANS THAT WINE LABELED 12.5 PERCENT CAN BE A DELICATE 11 PERCENT AND A WINE LABELED 14.9 PERCENT CAN ACTUALLY BE A CRUSHING 15.9 PERCENT.

18 HOW TO CULTIVATE YOUR SWEET TOOTH

Who can blame the countless conscientious objectors to sweet wine? Not only is it easy to erroneously assume that most off-dry or fully sweet wines are treacly sweet that they are at odds with today's focus on lighter, healthier fare.

When well made, a wine with some sweetness can be a wonderful addition to your vinous arsenal. Lightly sweet wines, like certain Rieslings and Chenin Blanc, have magical versatility with food, echoing the sweet tastes and taming the spice that appears on our increasingly eclectic table.

And it's not that winemakers are adding doses of extra sugar, as often happens with the inferior stuff. Instead, they come by sweetness naturally, typically by using extra-ripe grapes and stopping fermentation before all of the grape sugar converts to alcohol.

But for those who maintain that it is just not their thing, I hear you, and rest assured that not even I drink sweet wine with passionate regularity. In fact, in chapter 20 I reveal how you can entirely bypass the issue of sweetness in your appreciation of Riesling.

You owe it to your palate to give sweet wine another chance. In fact, you might actually already have a sweet tooth without knowing it. It is a wine industry maxim that consumers "think dry but drink sweet." How else can you explain the continuing popularity of off-dry styles of Prosecco or Coca-Cola or Snapple?

Heed the wisdom of Steve Jobs, who once said of the Apple Macintosh that "people don't know what they want until you show it to them," and ask a trusted merchant or savvy sommelier to lead you to quality wine with a bit of sweetness. Unlike a mai tai or other ungainly confection11, it will balance its sweetness with a wash of vibrant acidity. Find a wine that worships at the altar of acidity, and focus your mind on that invigorating tanginess when you are drinking it, and you may just find yourself hopelessly seduced by sweet.

19 RIESLING CAN PLEASE THOSE WITH A NOSE FOR EXXON

Nail polish, floor wax, magic markers, a new tennis ball. We're not supposed to like these seemingly noxious smells, but many of us do. My noxious odor of choice is gasoline, its hot fumes inducing in me a second or two of accidental euphoria. Perhaps I grew up passing one too many refineries on the New Jersey Turnpike; then again, if it did not hurt so good, why would illustrious fragrances such as Bvlgari Black and Guerlain Shalimar be known for evoking a hint of gasoline?

The good news for my fellow gasoline-philes is that there is a wine that offers similar aromas in certain bottles. It is Riesling, and it is one of the scents I look forward to in wine made from this still underappreciated grape. The gasoline smell tends to show most often in aged or markedly ripe Rieslings. It is usually subtle and one of several notes we would expect of Riesling, such as flowers, lemons, stone fruits, and minerals. When it is too pungent and eclipses the wine's other aromas, most would consider this a flaw.

Scientists have identified the naturally occurring chemical compound responsible for Riesling's high-octane charm, as they have for many of wine's desirably dangerous scents (chapter 105). Some smell it as kerosene or paraffin or even vinyl, but if identifying it as such would disenchant your guests, do what we insiders do and use the euphemistic and British term "petrol." If that still is too crude, so to speak, the French language will save the day with the elegant "*goût de pétrole*."

20 HOW TO DISCRIMINATE AGAINST SWEET RIESLING

To achieve the highest level of wine hipster-dom today, you are supposed to have rapturous regard for Chenin Blanc from the Loire, obscure wines of France's Jura region, Sherry of all types, and—the original oeno-geek pinup—Riesling.

While I don't quite possess the unwavering adoration for Riesling that I see in its impassioned disciples, I do appreciate its feathery light body, delicate flavors, and affordable complexity. It is also comes as a revelation to many novices that Riesling doesn't have to be sweet, which is a reflexive assumption that will keep the grape more of an art-house affair than a summer blockbuster for most of us.

So for the legions of people who mistakenly assume that all Riesling is sweet, I offer this divining rod to refreshingly dry styles:

DEPENDABLY DRY

AUSTRALIAN RIESLING: lemon-lime, minerally, floral, ultra-crisp character, especially from producers mostly in the Claire and Edna Valleys
Try: Annie's Lane, Grosset, Jacob's Creek, Jim Barry, Leasingham, Lindeman's McWilliam's, Penfolds.

AUSTRIAN RIESLING: citrusy and steely, notes of green apples or pears, often with concentrated, intense flavors; often weightier and more expensive than Australian and dry German Riesling
Try: Alzinger, Bründlmayer, Domäne Wachau, Hirtzberger, Schloss Gobelsburg.

SOMETIMES DRY

GERMAN RIESLING: can range from sweet to resolutely dry, the latter of which even German consumers now tend to favor; for the driest, look for the work "Trocken" on the label, which, frustratingly, isn't always used
Try: Dr. Loosen, Gunderloch, J.J. Prüm, Robert Weil, Selbach-Oster.

AMERICAN RIESLING (ESPECIALLY WASHINGTON STATE; FINGER LAKES, NY; CALIFORNIA): some are semisweet, so look for "dry Riesling" on the label
Try: Château Ste. Michelle (Washington State), Dr. Konstantin Frank (Finger Lakes), Hermann J. Weimer (Finger Lakes), and Trefethen (Napa).

ALSATIAN RIESLING: usually richer than German Riesling, and often dry or just a touch sweet, with subtle notes of peach or apricot; can sometimes seem sweet when in fact its sugar content is restrained
Try: Hugel, Kreydenweiss, Ostertag, Trimbach.

"*If the Germans like [Riesling], how sweet can it be?*"
—*Peter Scolari's character on the HBO series Girls*

Celebrating 1982—the wine and the band (Loverboy) of that vintage—at my Aspen Food & Wine seminars.

F C

A

W

O D
D
E

PART
4

10% Alc. By Vol.

21 LAUGH AT OVERLY SPECIFIC WINE AND FOOD PAIRINGS

I am always amused when certain wine writers recommend that a particular wine type should be paired with a highly specific dish, giving us the impression that it, and only it, is the acceptable pairing. What goes with New Zealand Pinot Noir? Duck in salt crust with a lingonberry emulsion, of course. What must we eat with that Pinot Grigio? Poached whelk with brine of fiddlehead fern.

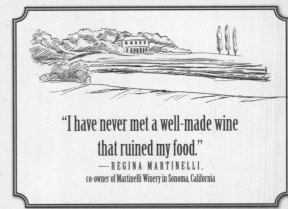

"I have never met a well-made wine that ruined my food."
—REGINA MARTINELLI, co-owner of Martinelli Winery in Sonoma, California

Fetishistically precise pairings could not be more misleading to the wine-drinking public. The simple fact is that wine and food are far more versatile with each other than some experts let on. In a wine culture permeated by anxiety about making the wrong decision, it should come as a relief to know that it is difficult to run too far afoul when marrying food and wine.

In fact, when it comes to middleweight wines, virtually anything goes. This includes most sparklers and medium to full whites such as Californian Sauvignon Blanc and restrainedly oaky Chardonnay, as well as light to medium reds such as Beaujolais, Pinot Noir, and lighter-style Rioja and Chianti. Rosé is also a mainstay of the middle ground. All of these are what I call pivot wines, meaning that they easily straddle the foods we associate with white wines and those we associate with red. They flatter almost everything.

Where we should do a bit more thinking is at the extremes of weight. So with delicately light-bodied wines like Pinot Grigio, we look to lighter preparations such as shellfish, spring vegetables, and dishes with citrus sauces. A pot roast, on the other hand, would hijack your perception of such a light wine. Conversely, a rich-style Zinfandel calls for similarly weighty foods, such as short ribs, lamb chops, or preparations in rich or dark sauces. Our sturdy Zin, on the other hand, would bully the flavor of a mild white fish or delicate soup.

When you learn to approximate the weight of food with the weight of the wine, you have mastered most of what is truly critical about food and wine pairing. There are of course certain affinities and hazards that we will discuss in the coming chapters. But the next time you read that a particular Merlot urgently calls for braised peacock with handmade filindeu noodles, give a knowing chuckle and turn the page.

22 YOU CAN COLOR COORDINATE FOOD AND WINE

Who hasn't come across the outdated directive to serve white wine with white meat and red wine with red meat? Sure, it's easy to remember, but its myriad exceptions render it virtually useless today.

Instead, the soundest advice is the try to match the intensity or weight of the dish with that of the wine. This more relaxed advice allows for combinations such as seafood with red wine that would never pass muster with the old white-with-white maxim.

There is an even easier way to think of food and wine pairing—that is to match them as you would clothes in your closet or paint in your home. What I mean is that there is a secret color-coding system such that certain hues of wine often have an affinity for similar colors in food. I cannot tell you exactly why, but it is a little-known and surprisingly effective shortcut to pairing success:

Green foods: Green salads, vegetables, and herbs pair well with whites that are so light that they seem to show a tinge of green, such as Sauvignon Blanc or Vinho Verde from Portugal. They also go well with wines that have a subtle green note in their character, such as the herbal notes in Grüner Veltliner from Austria or Albariño from Spain.

Pink foods: So pleasing is rosé with blushing seafood like tuna, salmon, and lobster, as well as similarly hued meat such as ham and hot dogs, that I've long called pink-with-pink my "rule of P."

Yellow foods: All manner of egg dishes, as well as yellow produce such as corn and pineapple, connect beautifully with richer, golden whites such as Chardonnay, Viognier, and Sémillon. The often-oaky flavors of Chardonnay are a slam-dunk with the creaminess of butter sauces.

Dark foods: Red meats of the dark persuasion, including steak, lamb, and game, have a natural affinity with dark, full-flavored red wines such as Cabernet Sauvignon, Syrah, and Malbec. Deeper-hued sauces, including bordelaise and peppercorn, as well as techniques that lend a darkening element, such as grilling and blackening, only add to the harmony that these foods have with inky-red wine.

> "MY FRIENDS FAIL TO FOLLOW ANY RULES WHEN IT COMES TO PAIRINGS. A COMMON DISCUSSION IS WHAT STRAIN OF SATIVA BEST ACCENTUATES GRÜNER VELTLINER."
> —SAM SPENCER, CO-OWNER AND HEAD WINEMAKER, CALIFORNIA'S HIGH HEAD WINES

23 REDS *CAN* SWIM WITH THE FISHES

Ever since the book *Red Wine With Fish* was published twenty-five years ago, gastronomes in the know have been happily wolfing down their *poisson* with a lively red. And yet old rules die hard, especially when they are perpetuated by pop culture. Take *Parks and Recreation*'s moody Craig Middlebrook, who while auditioning to be a sommelier, hilariously exclaims, "What kind of monster orders red with fish?!" Even James Bond has dissed the pairing, when, in *From Russia With Love,* he confirms the villain's identity by noticing his seemingly poor taste: "Red wine with fish. Well, that should have told me something."

British secret agents notwithstanding, red wine can be delightful with seafood, especially when the red is relatively light bodied, crisp, and low in tannin. The reach-for choice is a light-style Pinot Noir, which is why Oregon Pinot and fresh salmon is as classically Oregonian as the old-growth forests and bearded bartenders. You get a gold star if the salmon is grilled or wood smoked, as Pinot's lightly oaked cherry-spice profile flatters the smoke kissed. It need not be salmon, either. Any rich, oily fish, such as tuna, trout, or mackerel, has the intensity to stand up to a lighter red. An accompanying savory or earthy sauce, such as one featuring mushrooms, will build an even stronger bridge to a red wine.

Pinot Noir is just the launchpad, as lighter, tangier styles of Rioja, Chianti, and even Zinfandel fit the bill, as do exotic delicate reds, such as ones from the Loire, Blaufränkisch from Germany, Zweigelt from Austria, and the sommelier-darling, Poulsard from France's Jura region.

But can oysters and shellfish join our harmonious voyage on the red sea? A hearty "aye" to that, though the dour-minded find that matching them with red wine can sometimes leave an unpleasant tinfoil sensation in the mouth. That may be the case with hefty, tannic reds, but slurp your Beausoleil oysters with a chilled, svelte, low-tannin Beaujolais and your sailing will be smooth.

24 WHITES HAVE A BEEF

Although few combinations are as pleasurable as a juicy sirloin with a rich, mouth-coating Cabernet Sauvignon or Barolo, it is time to send the "only red wine with red meat" limitation to slaughterhouse once and for all. The rule starts to break down as early as the appetizer course. Charcuterie such as bresaola and soppressata are perfectly toothsome with a range of white wines, their accompaniment of lemon or capers making them candidates for even light, zingy pours like lemony Sauvignon Blanc.

Most red meat, however, calls for a richer white wine, one with the weight to stand up to the intensity of meat. This often means a creamy, oaked-up white, though one with enough acidity to cut through the richness of the meat. If you can't tell where I'm going with this, then allow me to spell it out: Chardonnay. Buttery, New World styles with prominent acidity are the pull-the-level choice, as are tangier versions of white Burgundy, which have the advantage of often possessing a wet-rocks stoniness that matches the funky minerality of steak and lamb chops. Take it from me: rich, sprightly Pugliny-Montrachet with minerally porterhouse is one of life's great exhilarations.

Other meat-greeting whites include zesty-style Rhône whites (their oily texture mirroring the likes of beef stew), Viognier and white blends from California's Paso Robles (which make fast friends with burgers), and even relatively rare aged Sémillon from Australia, its smoky, tropical profile a pleasing partner with chorizo. If you really want to blow minds, find some aged, dry Riesling, whose hefty flowers and petrol character can flatter everything from steak tartare to hearty game dishes.

25 DO NOT LIMIT VEGGIES TO WHITE

Who can blame the veggie-minded for being blinded by the white? The generally tangy, lighter, sometimes herbal nature of white wine is the logical accompaniment to foods of leafy, stemmy, and rooty persuasion.

Mouthwatering renditions of Chablis, Grüner Veltliner, Sauvignon Blanc, and Vermentino are the no-assembly-required match with everything from avocado toast to pesto sauce. Even veggies such as asparagus and artichokes that are difficult to match because of their uniquely dominating flavor play nice in the presence of a steely, zippy white.

However, the medium weight and habitual savoriness of rosé makes it just as good of a bedfellow with vegetables as white wine. Think of all the veggie-oriented dishes that arise from rosé's spiritual homeland of Provence, such as ratatouille, tapenade, onion tarts, salad, and the truffle omelette.

Moving down the color chart, be sure not to give short shrift to red wine. A pinnacle partner is Chinon and other reds from France's Loire Valley, because they are often only light to medium bodied and have a green, herbal dimension that mirrors those in vegetarian dishes. The typically light and earthy quality of Beaujolais and Blaufränkisch from Austria is going to show well with vegetables. Don't stop there: consider the acidic Chianti with tomato-focused preparations, edgy Dolcetto with kale and other bitter greens, woodsy Pinot Noir with mushrooms, and earthy Rioja with lentils.

Vegetarians need not give up on bolder reds, either. Winter vegetables like squash and eggplant, bold cheeses such as Parmesan and Gouda, and deeply flavorful roasted or caramelized vegetables all have the intensity to stand up to a Cabernet Sauvignon or a Malbec.

Are your know-it-all friends telling you that a robust Brunello or Portuguese red is too big for meatless preparations? Prove them wrong by dishing up a luscious mushroom risotto.

26 BETTER TO BE AN INTERNATIONALIST THAN AN INDIGENIST

In our locavore age, the pairing of regional ingredients with local wine has never been more stressed, justifying the timeworn advice of wine experts that "what grows together, goes together." I, too, am a believer and would never turn down the spot-on deliciousness of Oregon salmon with a Willamette Valley Pinot Noir or Argentinean Malbec with gaucho-grilled steaks. This is doubly true for time-tested European matches, be it Sancerre with Loire Valley–made chèvre, local Lambrusco with the salumi of Emilia Romagna, or Fino Sherry with Serrano ham in Spain. How can you doubt the wisdom of centuries of experience?

Yet with our brave new world of wine now in full flower, the indigenous approach is not always the guiding light it once was. With compelling wine from so many new and rediscovered locales, it should be only one option among a glorious many, one trusty bullet in your gastronomic holster. More fruitful for the modern gastronaut is to take advantage of a veritable United Nations of possible matches. This is the time for Vinho Verde from Portugal with Thai ground chicken, Chianti with spicy gumbo, Sonoma Coast Pinot Noir with coq au vin, and other bliss-bringing, cross-cultural alliances. Traditional pairings will never go out of style, but there is now too much opportunity not to zigzag liberally across territorial lines. See (chapters 36 and 37) for even more of my favorite pairings.

Not only are there more options and flexibility in an internationalist approach, but there is a certain stirring satisfaction in getting seemingly disparate cultures to play nice together, even if it is just at the dinner table. It wasn't long ago that I was in Sydney and realized that my dinner represented no less than four continents. I proudly tweeted: "It's good to be a Yank savoring Spanish wine with Szechuan food in Australia."

27 SOME REDS CAN TAKE THE HEAT

Peruse the list of any wine-knowledgeable Indian or Chinese restaurant and you will see a preponderance of whites such as German Riesling, Gewürztraminer, and Chenin Blanc. This is because whites with a bit of sweetness have long been known to cool down the scorches of a chili-laden curry or Szechuan beef, much like a sweet mango lassi quenching spicy samosas or a frozen margarita taming the heat of a piquant salsa. White with spice is sage advice, except when the wine is excessively oaky, as with some Chardonnay, or has relatively high alcohol content, as in many Gewürztraminer. Both oak and alcohol can accentuate the heat in spicy dishes, making what would otherwise be a spice-welcoming white lose its cool.

But what about reds? Many gastronomes fear serving red with spice because a tannic, gum-drying red such as Cabernet Sauvignon or Syrah intensifies the sensations of heat in your mouth, jangling your nerves like Courtney Love screeching into a broken microphone. But there is no reason to be a complete rougeophobe when the heat is on. The magic comes when you choose a lighter-bodied, amply fruity, low-tannin red such as a Beaujolais (see page 37), a lighter-style Barbera from Italy, or a Pinot Noir. (It should be noted that rosé also operates in a similarly smooth, versatile fashion and thus has comparable powers of refreshment.) When chilled and willing, these lighter reds can provide as much cooling relief as any of the famously firefighting whites.

28 DRINK BUBBLY THROUGHOUT (OR EVEN AFTER) A MEAL

Most of us are like twitchy squirrels when it comes to consuming Champagne and its more affordable cousins (see page 49), storing it up for special occasions or using it as an aperitif rather than treating it like the willing flavor and mood booster that it is.

In fact, insiders not only enjoy bubbly more freely; they drink it *throughout* a meal. Dry versions play nicely with almost any savory dish and have a natural affinity for salty tastes such as nuts, olives, and soy sauce, as well as for fried miracles such as calamari and pommes frites. Its cold temperature and moderate alcohol will also take some of the "pow" out of kung pao chicken and other spicy fare, as I elaborate on in the next chapter.

But what about bubbles after a meal? It often surprises drinkers that many major Champagne houses make semisweet (labeled "demi-sec") or fully sweet (i.e., doux) styles, which—in contrast to today's penchant for dry bubbly—was the dominant style of the nineteenth century. My favorites, Taittinger Nocturne and Veuve Clicquot Demi-Sec, will send you off into the night with sweet sparkle.

Even better, and more consistent with today's calorie consciousness, is to serve *dry* Champagne at the end of a meal. Wine pros have traditionally discouraged people from doing this because a sweet dessert such as apple pie and a dry wine like brut Champagne tend to clash on the palate. But there's no reason why you can't enjoy a dry Champagne with a lightly sweet dessert or, even better, as a palate-cleansing meal ender in itself. It is the wine equivalent of a refreshing lemon sorbet. I tell my audiences that one of the great pleasures is giving a meal "Champagne bookends."

29 SPARKLERS RULE WITH SPICY FOOD

We've covered which whites and reds work best with spicy food, but if I had to make a desert-island pick for the *caliente* calibrated, one choice would stand out: sparkling wine.

"You *can't* be serious," I hear the fusty traditionalist scold me with his best McEnroeian indignation. "Bubbly is for tuxedo-clad elegance and celebration; it is not supposed to ride sidesaddle on sriracha-fueled feeds and food-truck fiestas."

Au contraire, my fustafarian: as we become ever more adventurous and eclectic, the time has come for sparkling wine to loosen its tie and acknowledge one of its greatest functions—being a sprightly and soothing accompaniment for spicy food. Think of what we normally want to drink with jungle curry or Caribbean jerk chicken or African lamb merguez: a frosty mug of beer. Sparkling wine, with its coldness and restrained alcohol content, operates with similar powers of mollification. Its bubbles also provide a refreshing contrast and palate-cleansing lift to the vindaloo-victimized tongue.

Does this mean you should blow that nuance-filled bottle of Krug on your next hot sauce-bathed feeding frenzy? Probably not, because it is better to serve simpler bubbly such as Prosecco, Cava, or Cremant (page 49), so you don't have to worry about the heat numbing your perception of Champagne's subtleties. Then again, one of my all-time favorite pairings was at a party where the host dared to serve rosé Champagne with chili-laced spare ribs.

30 CHAMPAGNE GOES WITH EVERYTHING

In one of my recent seminars, an audience member asked me when is the best time to drink Champagne. I responded unapologetically, "Always." Laughter ensued, and I then found myself leading an unplanned call-and-repeat chant:

"Champagne when?" I hollered.

"Always!" they answered.

We went back and forth several times as if we were cheering on our favorite football team to the brink of victory.

And in a way, we were. In the sport of happiness, there is no greater franchise than Team Champagne. What other beverage is universally used for celebrating victory, christening boats, or even baptizing newborns (chapter 96)?

Beyond its formidable celebratory powers, Champagne (and other sparkling wine) is among world's the most versatile beverages, so much so that I have devoted a chapter to why you should drink it throughout a meal and even why it also deserves to be a meal ender (chapter 28). Its crackly acidity harmonizes with the salty, contrasts with the creamy, provides lift to anything fried, and cools off the spicy. Its often-yeasty character makes fast friends with mushrooms, eggs, and other earthy flavors. There is nothing better with the seafood and soy sauce of Japanese food. You can dress it up with caviar, truffles, or foie gras, or go casual with popcorn or Cheez Doodles. If there is ever doubt, remember that Champagne's versatility makes it wine's equivalent of "green eggs and ham": you can drink it on a plane, you can drink it in the rain.

I can hear wine's brooding Betties ask: what about heavier foods such as steak or stew? As rock legend Robert Plant might answer, the song remains the same: "*Always* Champagne." While such pairings run the risk of eclipsing bubbly's relatively delicate taste, it nevertheless has a built-in get-out-of-jail-free card: its bubbles. Not only is such effervescence scientifically proven to get you buzzed faster, their inescapably uplifting effect spur you to disregard the rules.

31 WHITES ARE BETTER WITH CHEESE

Opting for the less predictable pairing of white wine is much like director Mike Nichols's choice of Dustin Hoffman for the lead in *The Graduate:* not many directors would think to cast a pale, diminutive actor in a role that originally called for a bronzed alpha male, but Nichols's decision turned out to be a masterstroke.

Few people, of course, are going to cry, "Cut," if you continue to serve sturdy reds like a Californian Cabernet with a cheese platter. Reds with cheese is as much a time-honored pairing as coffee and doughnuts or Cheech and Chong. With good reason: when the notion was propagated many years ago, red wines generally tended to be lower in alcohol and thus more able to refresh the palate. And even today, big reds manage to harmonize with mild varieties like Parmigiano-Reggiano or dry cheddar, and they do an excellent job standing up to the pleasant stink of German Limburger, Italian taleggio, and blue-veined devils such as Stilton and Roquefort.

The problem comes when pairing hefty, dry reds with other commonly encountered cheeses. Enlightened eaters often find that the gooiness of Brie and Camembert, along with their moldy rinds, can make a dry red wine taste bitter. Instead, try a lighter, low-tannin red like Beaujolais or light-style Rioja. Even better, enlist a piercing, palate-cleansing white such as a Sauvignon Blanc or a sparkler, both of which will do much to foil a soft cheese's ooze. The same goes for a fresh cheese like buffalo mozzarella and acidic types like feta or goat cheese. A zingy, un-oaked white, such as Verdejo from Spain, or a vibrant American sparkling wine will match the tanginess of such cheese without obscuring its flavor with vinous weight or tannin.

32 BLUE CHEESE AND SWEET WINE IS YOUR WORMHOLE

One of the great revelations that come with learning about wine is the astonishing compatibility of sweet wine with blue-veined cheese. It is like uncovering a new gastronomic universe: can a salty, pungent cheese like Roquefort really flatter a sweet, often honeylike or molasses-style wine?

Welcome to wormhole, my expeditionist. Sauternes, as well as the similarly apricot-inflected late-harvest Riesling, Hungarian Tokaji Aszú, and Canadian ice wine are pitch-perfect matches with moody blues such as Roquefort or Gorgonzola. If you crave a lighter pour, try off-dry Moscato d'Asti, although some might find that a creamy blue cheese bullies this feathery, fizzy wine. There will be no regrets, however, in dialing up a richer, fully sweet Port with a cheese like Stilton, a match as classically English as a Wimbledon curtsey.

The voodoo underlying this combination is a case of opposites attract—the edgy savoriness of the cheese harmonizing with the sweetness of the wine, not unlike a sprinkle of salt on chocolate or french fries with a milk shake. There's also a textural similarity at work, with the mouthfeel of a rich, creamy cheese mirroring that of a full-bodied, densely sweet wine.

33 DUNK COOKIES IN WINE

On a trip to Italy last year, I unintentionally broke all the rules. Pasta as a main course? I asked for it. Cappuccino after dinner? They shut that down. The most abominable crime came when I requested hot sauce at a pizzeria in Rome, which elicited a horrified "Americano, no, no no!" from an animated *pizzaiola*.

I came to appreciate that this normally free and easy country had strict food rules not for the sake of persnicketiness, but because of Italians' profound respect for ingredients and how they should be appreciated. Any lingering embarrassment I felt disappeared when I encountered another food tradition. But this one, happily, seemed more like a transgression: dipping biscotti cookies into Vin Santo, the Tuscan dessert wine whose name translates to "holy wine." There we were, at a cozy steak house in Florence, and well-sated diners were lingering over little glasses of this amber *vini dolci* and dunking slivers of almond biscotti into it. The nutty, caramelly wine saturated the crunchy biscotti, making them softer and memorably delicious.

So now we have our excuse for dunking cookies in dessert wine, all the better if the wine is Vin Santo, whose grapes are dried before fermentation to concentrate their sugars. But you can use any golden, apricot-y dessert wine—from an American late-harvest bottling to Canadian ice wine.

COOKIES 'N' WINE

34 DRIZZLE WINE ON YOUR DESSERT (AND EVEN PANCAKES)

Having established the pleasures of dunking cookies in wine, now let's consider the inverse: pouring wine *over* dessert. My apologies to wine's killjoys, but there is ample precedent here.

The most famous is to find a nice bottle of Pedro Ximénez Sherry, which is the sweetest, most syrupy form of Sherry (Pedro Ximénez is a grape, not a producer), and drizzle it on ice cream. Because Pedro Ximénez is so dark and sweet, chocolate ice cream is my choice, but you are free to experiment with other strong flavors such as rum raisin or espresso. You can also substitute a simple glass of sweet-and-thick Ruby Port or late-harvest Zinfandel, whose ripe berry flavors harmonize with stronger flavors of ice cream.

With more delicate flavors of ice cream, there is no reason why you cannot get drizzly with golden, medium-rich styles of dessert wine, including lighter late-harvest styles, the fortified Muscat de Beaumes-de-Venise from France, or the honey-and-orange-blossom pleasures of ice wine. The combination of sweet wine with ice cream synergistically creates its own swoon-worthy third flavor.

Ice cream need not be the only landing strip for dessert wine. In an experiment that is sure to drive a stake into the heart of every vintage-chart-memorizing snob, some friends and I convinced a collector to pour his leftover 1986 Château d'Yquem over our pancakes at breakfast one morning. With giddy mischievousness, we drizzled our flapjacks in this nectarous, ethereal dessert wine. It was a smash hit, winning over even the collector. An engineer in the group made the pairing even better by suggesting that we apply a "butter barrier" on the pancakes to prevent the Sauternes from fully absorbing into the cake. Yquem on pancakes has since become an annual devil-may-care tradition.

35 CHOCOLATE WITH WINE ISN'T THE DISASTER THEY SAY IT IS

To hear certain pros speak of the pairing of wine and chocolate, you would think that the commingling of the two was as wise as letting Ozzy Osbourne take custody of a white dove. It is as if in the early days of wine education, one cranky expert set a rule against it, and almost every subsequent sage has dutifully fallen into line. My reaction is this: when I look around a restaurant and see so many people finishing their wine with chocolate cake, I do not see a lot of frowns.

To be sure, if you are having the ghost of Julia Child over to your place for an evaluative dinner, you might want to avoid pairing lighter, tangy styles of wine, especially dry whites, with chocolate because the sharpness of the wine and the sweetness of the chocolate tend to clash on the palate, creating a sour effect for many people. And chocolate is so flavorful and mouth-coating that in many cases its intensity will eclipse the flavors in your wine. This is why the only vinously correct wines for chocolate are deeply flavorful dessert wines like Port, Banyuls from southern France, and sweet styles of Madeira. The thinking goes that you don't want your dessert to outsweet your wine.

But do we really need such precision here? Most red wines may not be as intense as chocolate, but many, I think, are rich enough that they will not distract you from the opportunity to enjoy two of life's great indulgences together. And many reds see enough contact with oak barrels such that they themselves receive an impression of sweetness, thereby building enough of a bridge to chocolate. Marry a rich, not-too-dry, not-too-special Malbec, Shiraz, or Zinfandel with that nugget of Valrhona? Magic 8 Ball says: "As I see it, yes."

Those who would ban wine and chocolate are a bit like the precious snowflakes who avoid Champagne and caviar because the combination can taste a bit metallic. In both cases, if you are lucky enough to be served the combination, try not to overthink it; relax and enjoy your good fortune. And if you can't bring yourself to do so, wait there: I'll have yours.

36 UNEXPECTEDLY SUBLIME PAIRINGS

Chablis with oysters, Fino Sherry with almonds, red Burgundy with roast chicken, smoky Zinfandel with barbecue—if you want to get a wine enthusiast hot and bothered, just whisper a classic food and wine pairing in his or her ear. Even better, do it with two wineglasses in tow and an Eartha Kitt purr in your voice.

What many people do not realize, however, is that there is a world of surprisingly delectable pairings beyond the conventional, ones that cross territorial and gustatory lines in a manner befitting the multifariousness of modern eating. Let's examine the best of them:

BUBBLY + PIZZA

A pairing of two of life's indispensables, the acidity in a sparkler such as a Napa bubbly, Cava, or Prosecco cutting through the cheese and harmonizing with the piquancy of the tomato sauce.

BUBBLY + SALT-AND-VINEGAR POTATO CHIPS

How can you not drool when you contemplate this tangy-on-tangy match?

BUBBLY + FRIED CHICKEN

The cleansing bubbles and acidity of sparkling wine are tailor-made for the crispy, greasy delights of fried chicken. It's not surprising that there are now eateries devoted to "birds and bubbly"; I even taught a seminar on the subject at the South Beach Wine & Food Festival.

ENGLISH SPARKLING WINE + GLAZED COCKTAIL SAUSAGES

Your taste buds will rearrange themselves into the shape of a Union Jack in appreciation of Brit fizz with crispy, glazed little sausages.

VINHO VERDE + THAI MINCED CHICKEN

The inexpensive, fizzy, almost beerlike Vinho Verde operates like a ceiling fan on the blazingly hot, delightfully greasy Thai dish.

ARNEIS + LOBSTER ROLL

Italy via Maine never tasted so good: tangy, peachy Arneis from Italy readily snuggles up to a creamy, succulent lobster roll.

NEW ZEALAND SAUVIGNON BLANC + XIAO LONG BAO (CHINESE SOUP DUMPLINGS)

The energetic, citrusy Sauvignon Blanc provides pitch-perfect refreshment to the broth-borne earthiness of pork soup dumplings.

AUSTRALIAN RIESLING + FISH AND CHIPS

Not only does a penetratingly dry and vibrant Aussie Riesling give lift to fried morsels on your plate, but the accompanying vinegar also works with this dry, tart style of Riesling.

OFF-DRY RIESLING + HONEY MUSTARD PRETZELS

The sweet-sour nature of the pretzels flatters that of the Riesling, creating a gastronomic synergy of the Bavarian kind.

CHARDONNAY + POPCORN

The creamy Chardonnay meets its match in the equally buttery popcorn and the wine's acidity finds favor with the popcorn's saltiness

CHARDONNAY + KRAFT MACARONI AND CHEESE

The butteriness of a rich Chardonnay from California or Australia adores the creaminess of this comforting classic.

CHARDONNAY + GRILLED STEAK

You'd better believe it: a richer, toasty-style Chardonnay can bring all sorts of love to the rich, charred aspect of steak.

ALBARIÑO + BURGER

The weight of a richer-style Albariño stands up to the meaty goodness of a burger. Albariño tends to have ample acidity, which will keep your mouth refreshed and ready for the next beefy bite.

ROSÉ + BAREBECUE POTATO CHIPS

Dry and pink goes with everything but reaches the thin-air heights of greatness in the presence of barbecue potato chips.

ROSÉ BUBBLY + GREEK YOGURT

I accidentally discovered this unforgettable match late one night when on a whim I poured a bit of sprightly, fruity rosé Prosecco into a half-eaten cup of black cherry frozen yogurt. The angels sang.

RED BORDEAUX + ENCHILADAS

Until I saw a daring group of wine connoisseurs host a Bordeaux and enchiladas party, I had no idea these two elements were so compatible.

The pairing works best with beef enchiladas and a simple, medium-bodied Bordeaux.

PINOT NOIR + PEKING DUCK

Ripe, cherry-inflected styles of Pinot Noir are besotted with game birds, and especially Peking duck—the smoky fruit of the wine harmonizing with the skin of the duck and its accompanying crispy plum sauce.

PINOT NOIR + GRILLED CHEESE SANDWICH

My friend Steve hosts an annual event during which various bottles of smoky, fruit-forward Pinot Noir from the Russian River are paired with delectable, crispy grilled cheese 'wiches.

CÔTES DU RHÔNE + KIBBE

Earthy, satisfying, unpretentious Côtes du Rhône crushes for Middle Eastern kibbe, the torpedo-shaped croquettes filled with bulgur and lamb.

ZINFANDEL + PEPPERED BEEF JERKY

Combining two of California's most savory passions—beefy, spicy jerky and meaty, peppery Zinfandel—will make your knees will knock with delight.

DRY LAMBRUSCO + DORITOS

This savory red bubbly cools down the spicy, umami-laden flavors in this beloved snack, while the bubbles cut through the chips' oily charisma.

MOSCATO D'ASTI + GLAZED DOUGHNUTS

The lightly bubbly and delicately sweet Moscato plays nice with the light and chewy character of glazed doughnuts.

AUSTRALIAN SPARKLING SHIRAZ + FROOT LOOPS

The intense berry character of this bubbly red provides a bridge to all manner of fruity foods, even that Saturday-morning bastion of unnatural fruit flavor, Froot Loops.

"Ordering pizza while drunk is like throwing yourself a surprise party."
—Unknown

750 ML   13.5% ALC. BY VOLUME

37 THE FRISSON OF HIGH-LOW

We are now seeing gastronomy steadily and gleefully merge the everyday with the sublime, whether it be Mario Batali allowing Zeppelin's "Whole Lotta Love" to growl over his Mint Love Letters With Spicy Lamb Sausage at Babbo or the ubiquity of restaurant high-low dishes such as truffled mac and cheese, cereal milk ice cream, and broccoli topped with Cheetos.

It is about time that we officially extended this approach to food and wine. Pairing special wine with humble food is lusty business, and it puts the emphasis exactly where it should be—on the wine. For your inspiration and delectation, the following are my most successful high-low marriages:

DELUXE CHAMPAGNE + FRENCH FRIES

My last supper would be simple: Champagne from Salon, a small producer of all-Chardonnay ("Blanc de Blancs" style in winespeak), with the sort of dark-gold, double-fried frites found at New York's venerable brasserie Balthazar. As Bryan Ferry (and later Gwen Stefani) croons: "More than this / You know there's nothing / More than this."

PRESTIGE CUVÉE CHAMPAGNE + POTATO CHIPS

No need to labor over preparing the classic Champagne accompaniment of French cheese puffs called *gougères*. Potato chips are a willing substitute, putting the sparkler's cleansing, salt-loving acidity to productive use.

SPECIAL CHAMPAGNE + JAMAICAN JERK CHICKEN

It was a decisive "ya, mon" when I poured the rich-style, nutty Veuve Clicquot La Grande Dame Champagne (in magnum) to serve with moist, meaty Jamaican jerk chicken from a local Caribbean eatery.

A TOP ROSÉ CHAMPAGNE + PIMENTO CHEESE

One of my most memorable festival pairings came when I matched Gosset rosé Champagne with chef Elizabeth Karmel's pimento cheese. A staple of Southern eating and a tradition at the Augusta National Masters Golf Tournament, creamy, spicy pimento cheese cottons to the cooling, cleansing effect of rosé Champagne.

SPECIAL ROSÉ CHAMPAGNE + RIBS

You will experience a fine endorphin rush pairing rosé Champagne with glazed baby back ribs, the cherry-inflected, smoky bubbly lifting the meat to greasy, glistening heights.

RARE SAUVIGNON BLANC + SCALLION PANCAKES

The humble, herbal Chinese appetizer attained the rank of swoon-worthy in the presence of Dagueneau Blanc Fume de Pouilly Silex, one of the world's best Sauvignon Blancs. The wine's crackling, lemon-and-thyme punch was the perfect platform for the fried, savory pancakes.

A TOP CALIFORNIAN CHARDONNAY + CHICKEN POT PIE

A veritable first-aid kit of comfort comes in the form of creamy, crusty, vegetable-laden chicken pot pie served with a lush, tropical fruit–inflected Chardonnay.

SPECIAL ROSÉ CHAMPAGNE + BURGER

A juicy burger may not be the reflexive choice when contemplating a partner for rosé Champagne, but pink bubbles have the weight, flavor, and power of refreshment to stand up to the salty, charred beefiness of a burger. The cherry, minerally miraculousness of rosé Champagne also meshes perfectly with ketchup and french fries.

A CRÈME DE LA CRÈME RED BURGUNDY + MARGARITA PIZZA

Few high-low pairings could match the bliss I experienced at a party at which a collector opened several vintages of La Tâche with freshly made pizza from a backyard pizza oven. The Burgundy's spicy, dried-cherry quality perfectly complemented the blistered disks of cheese and sauce.

UPSCALE PINOT NOIR + MEATBALL PIZZA

Biggie and Tupac could have achieved détente over this East Coast–West Coast pairing: succulent meatball pizza from New York's legendary Grimaldi's Pizzeria with the gorgeous, tangy, cherry-minty Williams Selyem Rochioli Riverblock Pinot Noir.

A FINE RED BORDEAUX + BURGER

It might have been a crime of desperation, but Paul Giamatti's character in *Sideways* was on to something when he drank his prized bottle of Château Cheval Blanc with a burger. The char of the burger is a magnificent match with the blackberry-focused, minerally charms of a fine Bordeaux.

FOOD AND WINE

UPSCALE CALIFORNIAN CABERNET SAUVIGNON + LICORICE

A Napa winemaker once clued me in to the mischievous fun of pairing Red Vines licorice with a similarly flavored, blackcurrant-y Cabernet, which I once demonstrated with bottles of Joseph Phelps Insignia during my seminars at the Aspen Food & Wine Classic. The key is to first drink the wine through the hole in the licorice stick and then devour the Cabernet-saturated stick as a culminating treat.

A SPECIAL BRUNELLO + SPAGHETTI BOLOGNESE

Spaghetti with a tomato-based meat sauce brings hedonic chills in the presence of the Sangiovese-based Brunello—the savory, dark fruit character of the wine integrating perfectly with the finely minced meats and vegetables that comprise a hearty Bolognese sauce.

TAWNY PORT + PEANUT BRITTLE

It was no less than a gustatory revelation when a sommelier enlightened me about the magic made by the joining of a smooth, orange-peel–scented Tawny Port with the nutty crunch of peanut brittle.

VINTAGE MADEIRA + PUMPKIN PIE

The crisp, burnt-toffee personality of sweeter styles of Madeira melds seamlessly with the spicy, creamy aspect of pumpkin pie.

VINTAGE MADEIRA + CRACKER JACKS

A surge of dopamine seized me when I opened a bottle of tangy 1933 (appropriately, the year Prohibition was repealed) Justino Henriques Madeira Malmsey along with a box caramel-coated Cracker Jacks.

SAUTERNES + CHEETOS

When a friend opened a finely aged bottle of Château d'Yquem, no one intended to defile this golden nectar with the presence of junk food. But a bag of Cheetos sat nearby, and before long we were reveling in the opposites-attract splendor of the salty, cheesy Cheetos with the marmalade and apricot flavors of the Sauternes.

SAUTERNES + PANCAKES

Another fine use of Yquem (1986, from a monstrous six-liter bottle) was to pour some on pancakes, as I describe earlier in this chapter . Moistening a plate of fluffy flapjacks with this marmalade-tinged elixir rates for me as one life's great accomplishments

PART

PRODUCT OF TH

BOTTLED IN

RESTAU

2 0

750 ML.
13% ALC. BY VOLUME

VE

NITED STATES

W YORK, NY

RANTS

1 3

REGAN ARTS, LLC

THE
LIST

NO. 0005

Mise en Bouteille au Domaine

13% ALC. BY VOL   PRODUCT OF NEW YORK   750 ML

38 SOME RESTAURANTS GOUGE BECAUSE THEY CAN

The need to cover glassware, staff wages, rent, inventory—the reasons are sundry for why wine is marked up an average of three times or 300 percent over the restaurant's wholesale cost, and sometimes much more than that. But to diners, wine pricing in restaurants seems less like money management and more like cash extraction.

It is true that many restaurateurs look lustfully to the wine list, and drinks menu, to goose their profits. The most egregious overchargers are able to do so in part because of the smoke screen that surrounds restaurant wine pricing, making price benchmarking difficult for the wine-buying public. It doesn't help that prices vary widely among restaurants of the same caliber; a Jordan Cabernet Sauvignon that sells for $80 at one eatery can be $120 at the chophouse down the street. The location and size of the establishment, of course, factor into the pricing, but sometimes the difference comes down to simply what the restaurateur thinks customers are willing to pay. And they know that we are willing to pay a lot when, at the table, we are a captive audience and in urgent need of a swig.

Adding to the shell game of wine pricing is the variance of markup in different price ranges. A restaurant that purchases a bottle for $5 wholesale can mark it up a dizzying 600 percent to $30 without most diners noticing. But to avoid inducing sticker shock, restaurants simply cannot pump up the higher end as much, so that Bordeaux purchased for $30 wholesale can be upped only 300 percent to $90. Confusing the situation even more is that few people outside of the industry have access to wholesale pricing lists, making it that much harder to discern a relative value from a flagrant fleecing.

But if you do have an idea of the wine's retail pricing, know that the general rule is that restaurants tend to mark up wine 200 percent over retail. Depending on the wine and the restaurateur's avariciousness, however, it can be inflated as much as four times what we pay in the store for it. It's enough to make you flip your ice bucket in disgust.

39 EVEN EXPERTS THINK WINE LISTS ARE A BERMUDA TRIANGLE

Only a sadistic game show host would give you mere moments to make one selection from hundreds of aggressively marked-up items for which the only information supplied on each was a price, a year, and a jumble of unfamiliar words. Yet that is what we are asked to do each time the wine list is deposited in our hands. It might be a relief to know that even experts view the wine list as a Bermuda Triangle—a treacherous zone that defies mastery for even the most skilled operators.

Before we discuss how to navigate this perilous air space, let's look at the two factors that make the wine list such a flawed document. The first is the type of information it provides. The average list is no more than a mere price sheet, each entry no more than a terrifying number preceded by a mostly meaningless name. Far better is the list that accompanies each wine with a simple, interest-piquing description, such as "light-bodied, crisp white with notes of lemon and grass." Even if it fails to provide such elaborations, a list organized by major flavor sensations—"delicate and refreshing," "lush and fruity," and the like—constitutes a major improvement over the normally unilluminating document.

The quality of the information may be lacking, but most wine lists, to their detriment, do not lack for quantity. Though restaurants today do not favor the oenological *War and Peace* as much as they did in the past, most wine lists are still needlessly lengthy, in part because restaurants want to impress you with their sizable inventory and be perceived as a "serious wine restaurant" by critics judging these things. But like the Amazon shopper confronted with thirty-seven types of laundry detergent, people become overwhelmed with a surplus of selections. The best lists avoid the tyranny of overchoice, showing restraint by limiting themselves to 100 to 150 carefully considered options. The sommeliers writing wine lists would do well to remember the gist of Coco Chanel's secret to dressing well: before leaving the house, always remove one accessory.

40 EIGHT WAYS TO FIND RESTAURANTS THAT PLAY FAIR

Having examined the pecuniary and informational hazards of the modern wine list, let's now look at eight insider ideas for finding restaurants with fair wine pricing:

1 FOLLOW THE PROS.

Every city has certain restaurants favored by chefs and sommeliers, and these tend to be the ones with more reasonable wine markups. Follow them on social media or use Google to see where they are regulars.

2 AVOID HOTEL RESTAURANTS.

Whenever possible, bypass restaurants and bars in hotels. Catering to business travelers, wedding parties, and other free spenders, hotels often price their wines like they do that hamburger that somehow costs $40 through room service.

3 DON'T DISMISS THE UPSCALE CHAIN.

Restaurant chains like Hillstone and Legal Seafoods sometimes have surprisingly fair pricing because of the deep discounts they gain from purchasing wine in large volume.

4 SEARCH THE OLD STANDARDS.

Occasionally, a venerable, time-worn restaurant will forget to or refrain from marking up wine that it purchased years ago when prices were significantly lower. Their inaction is your bargain.

5 PREVIEW THE LIST.

Visit a restaurant's website before you go to see if they publish the list online, or contact the sommelier in advance and ask him or her to send you the list. Not only will they be most happy to do so, but also such homework will relieve you from having to neglect your tablemates in the moment.

6 CONSIDER THE VEUVE.

A good indicator of whether a restaurant is charging more or less than the standard for its location and caliber is to notice the price of a wine that appears frequently on wine lists. Veuve Clicquot Brut Champagne and Kim Crawford Sauvignon Blanc, both ubiquitous, are good gauges.

7 USE THE BEAUJOLAIS TEST.

Does the restaurant offer Beaujolais cru (see chapter 3), which is probably the best all-around value in restaurants, and do they price it reasonably? Unpretentious and still relatively unappreciated, Beaujolais cru should never cause sticker shock.

8 MAKE A CORKAGE CALCULATION.

Is the restaurant's corkage fee for BYO unusually high? If so, then they are probably similarly rapacious when pricing the wine.

When you BYO, it is wise to bring back-ups.

41 FIVE SHORTCUTS TO UNEARTHING THE LIST'S HIDDEN GEMS

Interested in strategies that anyone, even complete novices, can use to smoke out a wine list's hidden bargains? You've come to the right place:

1 ORDER THE UNPRONOUNCEABLE.

In general, the harder a wine is to pronounce, the less popular it is, because everyone is afraid to tackle its syllables. That lower demand often makes the wine a good value. Chardonnay gets marked up; Agioritiko from Greece, not so much. If you really want to say it properly, use your smartphone to Google its pronunciation. So important is this lesson that I even teach a seminar called "Hard to Say, Easy to Drink."

2 DISCOVER THE CHEF'S OR SOMMELIER'S GO-TO.

If the server seems knowledgeable and game, I will simply ask, "What does the chef or somm drink when she is off duty?" It tends to be something less obvious and affordably priced.

3 LOOK FOR AN OUTLIER.

If the list is short enough to get a quick overview, see if there is only one example of a certain type, such as a Falanghina from Italy on a mostly American list, or a New York State Riesling on a Eurocentric menu. This is likely a wine that the sommelier chose not out of thematic necessity but because he or she loves it and wants you to share his or her enthusiasm. Accordingly, it is often priced fairly to reward you for sharing his or her interest.

4 SEEK THE SECRET, OFF-LIST BOTTLE.

It can't hurt to ask your sommelier about what he or she is gaga about, adding, "even it if isn't on the list." Good sommeliers keep a secret stash of bottles that are no longer stocked or are set aside for favored customers. These wines often are from places where the somm has grown up or lived, so inquire about your somm's background to get the ball rolling. If your server takes a shine to you, he or she may just make that wine appear on your table.

5 THINK SPAIN.

No other major wine-producing country produces such a range of dependably delicious and affordable wines in every style. Bubbly? Cava, Txakoli from Basque country. White? So many, including the almost prime-time Albariño, the Sauvignon Blanc–like Verdejo, the up-and-coming Godello. Reds—the list is endless, from old friends such as Rioja and Ribera del Duero to the medium-weight Mencía from Bierzo to rich, plummy blends from Yecla, Jumilla, and Castilla y Leon.

42 FIVE WAYS TO AVOID THE LIST'S TOURIST TRAPS

Value on wine lists lies beyond the famous vineyards and marquee grapes. Here are five places to look in order to avoid the list's tourist traps:

1 EMERGING AND REDISCOVERED REGIONS:

There are now so many delicious, lesser-known grapes and regions available that it was the subject of my last book, *Oldman's Brave New World of Wine.* Whereas you will pay a premium for comforting likes of Chardonnay, Sancerre, Merlot, and Cabernet Sauvignon, it is much harder for restaurants to impose greedy markups on lesser-known gems such as Moschofilero or Gigondas. One easy way of homing in on these wines is to focus on hard-to-pronounce wines, as recommended on the previous page, or you can familiarize yourself with the best off-road choices on page 54.

2 BEYOND A REGION'S SIGNATURE WINE:

Value is also hidden in the long shadow cast by a region's signature wine. Instead of looking to Oregon for its duly famous Pinot Noir, try the state's arresting Pinot Gris; bypass the hyped-up Cabernet Sauvignon in Napa for its excellent but neglected sparkling wine; Chassagne-Montrachet is famous for its white wine, but its lesser-known reds offer delight at a discount.

3 NEGLECTED OR UP-AND-COMING NEIGHBORS:

Like the residents of New York's Sixth Avenue who enjoy the services and vibe of Fifth Avenue without having to pay the premium of living there, you should look to nearby areas that are either up-and-coming or unheralded. Try decently priced Savigny-lès-Beaune from Burgundy instead of its pricey and more famous neighbor Aloxe-Corton; consider California's less developed Anderson Valley instead of sizzling Sonoma for Pinot Noir; investigate Umbria's Sagrantino as an alternative to ambitiously priced Super Tuscans nearby.

4 BASIC OFFERINGS FROM CELEBRATED PRODUCERS:

Like ordering the lunch-only burger at Peter Luger Steak House, you can find a more basic offering from an esteemed source. It can provide some of the style and quality of the marquee offering but at a fraction of its cost. Wine-serious restaurants are especially fertile ground for the second- or third-string offerings of top producers. You might look for Bourgogne or village-level bottlings from a Burgundy star such as Domaine Leroy, a pinch hitter like Le Serre

Nuove from Super Tuscan house Tenuta dell'Ornellaia, or an everyday Côtes-du-Rhône from a storied producer such as Jean-Louis Chave.

5 AN OFF-YEAR OF A CELEBRATED WINE:

Despite my advice to largely ignore vintage (chapter 77), if you do find a prestigious bottle from a vintage year you know that to be unheralded, it will likely come at discount. This is because there are plenty of vintage-obsessed drinkers who will entirely dismiss a disappointing vintage, not realizing that the best producers can make great wine—through careful grape selection and skillful winemaking—even in poor vintages.

43 THE LIST MAY REWARD ADVENTUROUSNESS, OR THE SOMM'S PET WINES

A wine list is not put together by a gleaming, faceless Daft Punk robot, but by a living, breathing wine director or sommelier. Whether the list has 80 or 800 selections, if it is a good one, it needs to have enough familiar choices and reasonably priced bottles to keep from alienating the casual drinker. At the same time, in this age of unprecedented wine choice, many pros are justifiably excited about introducing diners to far-flung regions and little-known grapes.

This is where the treasure seeker wins. More often than not, a good wine list will include hidden choices of exceptional quality and extra-generous value buried in the orchard of their list like a few glisteningly ripe apples. These hidden picks tend to be overlooked types such as Txakoli from Spain's Basque country or a red from Portugal, the kind of alternative pours I describe in the Oldman's Ten Best rankings (Section 2), so make sure to familiarize yourself with them. The next time you are in a wine-friendly restaurant and see a well-priced wine from the Canary Islands or Slovenia, it's worth taking a chance on it; you might have found one of the list's Easter eggs.

In addition to rewarding the adventurous, some sommeliers like to underprice certain wines because they are personal passions. Not only is it human nature to want others to like what you like, but for sommeliers it is satisfying knowing that they are giving the stage, however briefly, to wines that they believe do not get it enough. These pet wines tend to be what I meant by outliers—i.e., standing out as unusual or incongruous in the context of the list, such as that small producer placed amid a bevy of big brands or that gently priced Barolo on a list full of southern Italian choices. Or it may simply be a grape or region that you don't see very often on any list, such as a Moroccan gem I recently encountered in Chicago.

44 CHOOSE THE CHEAPEST

If you scan a wine list like I do, then your eyes immediately fall to the least expensive wine, seeking refuge from extortionist prices that plague today's restaurants. But then, you think, you cannot totally cheap out, so you float up to the second or third least expensive choice. Here, we find the safely thrifty hovering above the ignominious floor of the bargain basement.

"Gotcha!" thinks the wine director with Dave Chapellean exuberance, having anticipated that you would alight upon this acceptably frugal choice. Knowing that it will sell swiftly, he may have slotted an overstocked bottle into this position on the list. Even worse, he may have marked up this wine more than any other, making it potentially the worst value on the list.

You are better served to order the cheapest wine, which diners often neglect out of fear of embarrassment and thus is often a better value. Just make sure you do so at a restaurant that cares about its wine, where even modestly priced wines are of admirable quality. These wines are often a personal favorite of the sommelier, such as the introductory wine of a favorite producer or a fine example from an unsung grape or region. When it comes down to it, any chimpanzee can peddle good wines that cost a fortune; truly talented sommeliers are able to find and sell deliciousness at the lowest end of the list.

So how do you know if you are in good hands at a particular restaurant? Look around: Does your server seem knowledgeable? Are there interesting wines by the glass—even though you should probably not order one (see the following page)? Does the wine list have thoughtful commentary? If so, then the bargain basement may very well be your penthouse suite.

45 AVOID WINE BY THE GLASS . . .

I call it "regret by the glass." Even when a friend and I resolve to have just one glass each, we will still often end up ordering another round. And that is exactly the reason wine by the glass sours like last month's sangria—because when the table is ordering four or more glasses (or, in some cases, just three), it is almost always less expensive to enjoy a whole bottle. Divide the price of a bottle by five, which is the number of five-ounce glasses that a standard bottle contains, and it becomes abundantly clear. Wines by the glass are so marked up that it is practically industry scripture that the cost of the first glass covers what that restaurant paid wholesale for the bottle.

The difference is not only monetary: opting for a bottle over a glass also gives you, of course, much wider choice, since you have the whole list at your fingertips. It also avoids the problem of the wine having gone stale or reds being served too warm, both of which are more likely due to that lonely preopened bottle sitting under the bar.

This is not to suggest that there is no place for by-the-glass selections. Some restaurants offer an exciting diversity of options, especially now that the Coravin device has made it possible to extract wine without having to pull the cork. If you are on an expense account, a few Coravin-caliber wines by the glass could make for a memorable evening.

I, however, prefer to treat wine by the glass like you would a travel-size purchase, confining its use to times of necessity, such as when ordering one or two aperitif or dessert glasses, or when one diner yearns for that extra glass after a bottle is finished. You could also make an argument for ordering by the glass when dining solo, but as you will read, there are good reasons to avoiding resigning yourself to this fate.

46 . . . BUT IF YOU CAN'T, ASK TO SPLIT THE GLASSES

If the thought of a green-visored restaurateur rapturously fingering your hard-earned money doesn't dissuade you from ordering wine by the glass, then there are ways of at least making the experience more rewarding.

First, you can ask your waiter for a taste to ensure that the wine is still fresh. Any restaurant worth its smoked sea salt will happily take back a glass that tastes less than optimal. If your concern is that the wine is not actually the varietal or producer you ordered, you can ask to see the bottle before it is poured. This might also discourage a restaurant from reusing another table's leftover bottle, a nefarious trick that is fortunately not terribly common in eateries wishing to stay in the good graces of diners and health codes.

In restaurants with strong by-the-glass menus, the real opportunity lies in exposing yourself to different types of wine. This is why you should ask your server for the wine equivalent of share plates: extra glasses that allow you to split each glass of wine. So a couple that each orders wine by the glass would end up with two half glasses. If you later crave more wine with your meal, that's another opportunity for each person to taste two more different half glasses. Not only does splitting each glass help justify the higher cost of wine by the glass by increasing the number of wines you can enjoy with your meal, such experimentation allows you to perform the all-important double fist (chapter 5)—i.e., tasting wines side by side to better appreciate the nuances among wine types.

47 ORDER A BOTTLE WHEN DINING ALONE

What is the solo diner to do? One glass is rarely enough for those with a healthy thirst, but a whole bottle is generally too much, although, as previously discussed, the latter's value for the money is much better if you foresee ordering multiple glasses. Sometimes the solution is a half bottle, which offers the diner about two and a half glasses, more than enough to raise a glass to yourself and wash away the mild unease of dining alone. But many restaurants do not offer half bottles or carafes, or quartinos for that matter, and when they do, the selection can be dreadfully sparse.

The way forward is clear: order a full bottle. No, I'm not advising you to *down* an entire bottle, unless it is an imbibing emergency and you keep well clear of a steering wheel. Many states now allow restaurants to recork or rescrew your bottle so that you can take it home, which is a fine, elegant solution.

But if leaving with your wine is not possible or desired, there is great satisfaction in gifting the remainder of your bottle to the staff. Simply slide it to your server or the bartender and with Bogartian swagger, tell 'em to "spread it around." And you were wondering how to speed the process of becoming a regular at that hot new restaurant?

Even more karmically rewarding is to offer your wine to another table. This can be so enriching that I still recall where (Sonoma), what (Radio-Coteau "La Neblena" Pinot Noir), and for whom (a sweet couple visiting from Atlanta) I first did this. A week later they tracked me down online and sent a delightful thank-you note. The best part of making such an offering is getting to decide the target of your largesse, as if you were piloting one of those roaming Publishers Clearing House trucks.

ORDERING
WINE

NO. 0006

Mise en Bouteille au domaine

13% ALC. BY VOL   PRODUCT OF NEW YORK   750 ML

48 USING A SOMMELIER REQUIRES ONLY THREE THINGS AND TINDER TENDENCIES

To locate a restaurant's sommelier or, in his absence, a knowledgeable server, I make the general inquiry, "Who here knows the most about the wine list?" It smokes out the wine mind while avoiding giving the waiter the impression he did not look polished enough to be the sommelier.

Then, to get the ball rolling, I say something like, "This is a great list, but a lot of it is unfamiliar. Can I get your help?"

A good sommelier can then guide you if you provide a mere three preferences: color, weight, and price. The threshold criterion, of course, is color—i.e., whether you want white, red, or bubbly. Then, narrow the field by whether you prefer a light or richer style, such as a light-bodied white or a full-bodied red. Finally, do not hesitate to specify a price range or a ceiling: "I'd like to spend up to $50 tonight." If you are too embarrassed to name a number, ask for wine that "won't break the bank" or point to a price on the list.

Those with wine knowledge might want to add a wild card factor. Narrow the field even further by specifying a quality that you tend to favor: earthy, oaky, smooth, or even the more open-ended "a lot of flavor" or "surprising in some way."

These criteria then go into the supercomputer that is the sommelier's brain, and she will start proffering choices that match your desires. The trick, I've discovered, is to resist the urge to immediately accept the first choice. Keep pressing the sommelier for suggestions from other regions and countries, scrolling through options as if you were thumbing through Tinder. "Sounds good. What else?" is the prompt I employ to keep the selections coming. This will give your sommelier the chance to recall other possibilities, and it will buy you time to consider the wines already offered. To tease the list out more, I'll sometimes ask, "Have you had this one?" which often elicits details on the wine that the sommelier never thought to volunteer.

After considering four or so options, it is time to go with your gut. In the event that all of the options sound equally alluring, ask for a few minutes and quickly search some of them on your smartphone. Or do what I do to break the tie: choose the name that sounds the coolest.

49 ASK FOR A SAMPLE

Although a discussion about wine possibilities can be immensely valuable, nothing surpasses the opportunity to actually test-drive a selection or two. Given an inquiry about a specific wine, smart sommeliers and servers offer a taste if it is available by the glass. "Do you want to try it?" is the skeleton key to my heart, a trust builder that makes me tip more generously and be more likely to return to the restaurant or wine bar.

Whether out of indifference or shortsighted frugality, too many servers do not think of offering a liquid preview. What rarely occurs to diners is that they can turn the tables and ask the sommelier for a taste of wine that is offered by the glass. The worst that she will say is no, but those possessing good business sense will foresee that such generosity can be mutually rewarding.

Of course, it matters how you ask to sample. Lest the somm assume that I am trolling for a freebie, I explain that a taste will help me decide among the excellent choices offered. If I am planning to order a bottle, which for me is pretty much a given, I tell a sommelier that, so she knows that a sizable purchase is in the offing. If she seems extra amenable, sometimes I will ask for tastes of two or three different wines so that I can choose from among them. Asking for a taste is also worthwhile when you are waiting for a table at the bar, which some restaurants do to get you to spend more money. Your request can neutralize this ploy and provide a holdover swig until your table is ready.

No matter the situation, everything seems to go smoother when I tell a sommelier or bartender that I desire "just a splash" and pinch my thumb and forefinger together—a lighthearted and nonconfrontational way of encouraging that person to make the extra effort.

50 ASK FOR A GOOD PRICE, NOT A GOOD VALUE

We have already established the potential reward of ordering the least expensive wine on a list (chapter 44). But how, actually, do we ask for it or other cost-conscious selections? Because of the societal taboo against talking about money, I used to try the indirect approach, asking for "a good value" or "a fair price" or something "easy on the wallet."

However, I have discovered that such barely disguised innuendo would often yield distressingly pricey recommendations, because—applying Clintonian semantic parsing—even expensive wines are good value if they drink like an even costlier wine. Although there are indeed *relative* good values in every price range, an empathetic server should know that someone with the guts to ask for "a good value" is probably not looking for a bottle in the middle to high range, even if that bottle punches above its weight in quality. While some servers honestly misconstrue your intentions, others might be hoping that embarrassment of making you spell it out will cause you to accept a pricier option.

Recently in New York, an eager server urged me to order an unremarkable $88 wine because "it had been marked down from $130." My reply: "That's like going from a triple mugging to a double mugging."

In any event, the way forward is to spell out your desires as unequivocally as Stanley's famous line "Did I stutter?" in *The Office*. Have no compunction about specifying a dollar amount as an upper limit, such as "I'd like to stay under $50." If such directness would unsettle your tablemates, just point to a price on the menu and ask for "something like that." If that is still too bold, go early to peruse the list and powwow with the sommelier before you sit down.

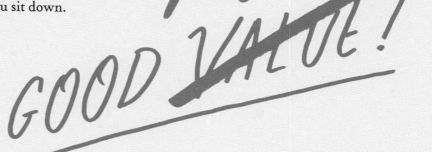

51 BEWARE THE BAD SOMM

As our dining culture has loosened up, wine service has become more enlightened and welcoming. Gone is the supercilious, ego-driven wine steward, his hauteur, disapproving manner, and sour breath matched by a surly insistence that patrons drink only *correct* wine types and producers.

All is not perfect in wine service, however, because the pompous sommelier has been replaced, in some precincts, by an equally vexing character: the self-indulgent sommelier overly focused on the obscure, the lucrative, or both. Smug is the new snooty; overconfidence, the new overweening. Tattoos have replaced the tastevin as the insider accoutrement, but like those outdated tasting dishes on chains, ink is not a proxy for hospitality.

Many modern sommeliers are doubtlessly competent and helpful, and some actually achieve the rarest of feats: making you feel knowledgeable. Heroic is the somm who helps you decide by presenting you with tastes of two different wines—such a light, fruit-forward Pinot Noir against a medium-rich, savory Chianti—just to learn what really moves you. A wine professional like this can take you to vinous places previously unfathomed.

All too often, however, the person charged with helping you select wine is aloof or indifferent. Recently, at a celebrity chef hot spot in New York, for example, the wine director emerged from the back office radiating impatient disdain. Her sulky stance and cursory recommendations made her seem like a cat poised to squirm away.

The inverse of the checked-out sommelier is the impassioned proselytizer. This character has a bottle to push, sometimes for no better reason than a need to move product that the restaurant has stocked in excess. In other situations, she will champion a wine not because she has deduced that it matches your preferences but because it agrees with hers. And a good sommelier has an instinctive feel for when to provide an interesting nugget about a wine or its winemaker, but avoids delivering a tableside soliloquy.

52 HOW TO AVOID GETTING "BANGED"

There's a fundamental conflict of interest in wine service: a sommelier's obligation to provide good service often runs counter to his or her need to maximize restaurant profits. Sommeliers are essentially the chief wine salespeople, and we cannot begrudge them that vital role in a world where wine profits often compensate for the losses incurred by the restaurant's food, labor, and real estate costs.

The hazard comes, however, when the sommelier or server puts profit margins ahead of sincere guidance, which can be particularly chafing given the vertiginous wine markups in many restaurants. You see this in something as common as the overfilling or topping off of glasses (chapter 59), that passive aggressive maneuver to compel you to order another bottle. It can also be seen when a sommelier gives scant attention to tables that appear frugal. Wine-oriented restaurants often keep track of which patrons are the big spenders, some even denoting them as "whales" or "ballers" in the reservation database. It is no secret that there are sommeliers who spend an inordinate amount of their time getting big spenders to "drop the hammer," while neglecting mere mortals like you and me.

Where the money issue becomes particularly dark is in the upsell, which is referred to by some industry insiders, unceremoniously, as "banging the guest." Sometimes a waiter will push a particular bottle that is "on sale" that night but is more than you wanted to spend. I typically resist the bait but will occasionally agree to it if the sommelier promises to take the bottle back if it is not to my liking. By making the sommelier personally guarantee her hot pick, you've minimized the risk for the potential reward of a memorable bottle.

More often, you encounter the upsell when you have established your price preference and the sommelier uses the social pressure of your tablemates to nudge you up to a pricier bottle. I call this the "lady and da lobster" maneuver, because it reminds me of when I once asked a waiter to recommend a few good tapas and he went straight for the entrée that was double the price of everything else. With the silky style of a tuxedoed Javier Bardem, the waiter turned to my girlfriend and declared, "The *LAY-dee*, I think she wants *da LAHB-ster*," mistakenly assuming that I was hostage to a first date.

The upsell also occurs when the wine you ordered has sold out, and the server recommends a substitute that exceeds the price of your desired bottle. In both this and the previous example, your best bet is to consciously uncouple from the exchange and navigate the list on your own.

High praise is owed to sommeliers who exhibit the opposite instincts, daring to downsell you to an equally delicious but less expensive choice. The willingness to downsell may be the single greatest indicator of a special sommelier, since it demonstrates with crystalline clarity that she has prioritized your interests over hers.

One Night Only "ON SALE" for ONLY $130

MONOPOLE
1962

FREDERICK
WILDMAN
AND SONS
NEW YORK CITY

SOCIÉTÉ CIVILE DU DOMAINE DE LA ROMANÉE-CONTI
PROPRIÉTAIRE A VOSNE-ROMANÉE (CÔTE-D'OR)

PRODUCE OF FRANCE

LA TACHE

APPELLATION · LA TACHE · CONTROLÉE

26.740 Bouteilles Récoltées

No 21046   L'ASSOCIÉ-GÉRANT

ANNÉE 1962   H. de V...

Mise en bouteille au domaine

53 HANDLING THE GLASSHOLE SOMM

Almost everything a server does either builds trust or depletes it. Once in a while, that trust isn't just diminished, it is eviscerated. I am not talking about run-of the-mill breaches in hospitality, such as when the server corrects your pronunciation or challenges your belief that a bottle is spoiled. Nor is it about an occasional act of carelessness, like the time a waiter allowed a bottle to slip from his hands on to the table's edge, where it shattered in a glittering star field onto my sweater.

No, we are talking about the foreseeably distressing. Take, for example, the diner at Bobby Flay Steak in Atlantic City who thought he had ordered a $37.50 bottle when his waitress told him it was "thirty-seven fifty." To the table's horror, it turned out to be a $3,750 bottle of Screaming Eagle, the rare cult Cabernet Sauvignon from Napa. After days of bickering back and forth, the restaurant eventually lowered the charge to $2,200, which is still a wicked price to pay for what sounds like an honest miscommunication. A savvier server would have asked for triple verification—or a signature in blood—before placing an order for such an outrageously expensive bottle.

And then there is the full-fledged glasshole. One need look no further than a recent piece in *The New York Times* in which a waiter at a Michelin three-star restaurant described how he and his fellow servers would play the "adjective game," competing to see who could sell diners wine with the "least helpful" descriptors possible; "haunted" was a favorite. In a follow-up article, a former waiter described how he and his co-workers were instructed to lie to a regular that he was getting his favorite Chardonnay by the glass when it was a totally different wine; the key, the waiter wrote, was to "sell people on your confidence."

If your sommelier seems to be a scoundrel of this sort, wrest back control and choose the wine yourself, but not before issuing a parting comment. Whether fussing over the perfect Windsor knot or Chanel jacket, sommeliers tend to be vain animals. At the same time, their job requires hauling wine, busing tables, and other dirty work that inevitably scuffs their footwear. So hit them where it hurts: ridicule their shoes.

Downsells you a delicious wine

Produces an off-the-list bottle

Happily brings you tastes to preview

Respects your desire for gently priced wine

Friendly and helpful about BYOB

Refrains from lecturing you

Listens carefully and steers you to choices that match your preferences

SOMMELIER
SAVIOR/SINNER
METER

Corrects your pronunciation

Overfills glasses; repours too quickly

Challenges your belief that the bottle is spoiled

Neglects you for "whales" or resents having to work the floor

Seeks to upsell you a more expensive bottle

Accidentally shatters a bottle on you

Brings $3,750 bottle when diner orders one for "thirty-seven fifty"

Lies to customers; ridicules their choices

REGAN ARTS, LLC

ANNÉE 2006

P. 120

DURING THE MEAL

No. 0007

Mise en Bouteille au Domaine

13% ALC. BY VOL   **PRODUCT OF NEW YORK**   750 ML

54 IGNORE THE CORK

When a waiter places a cork in front of me, I feel like a dog in a lab experiment. Put the challenge in front of Fido and see what he does. Maybe he will get it right.

Now hear this: Fido doesn't need to do anything. No need to sniff, bite, or bark at the cork. Treat the offer as a well-trained service animal would: ignore it. This is because the information you seek when you taste wine in a restaurant—to sniff and taste it for whether the wine has spoiled (chapter 69)—is far more accurate when you sniff the actual wine rather than the piece of tree bark the bottle has been plugged with.

While most experts agree with my stance, cork fondlers still persist in the wine wilds. Some like to feel the cork for excessive dryness or inhale it for unpleasant smells, though both cases are hardly conclusive of a flawed wine. Others will use the cork to verify a wine's authenticity, matching the cork's markings to the label on the bottle. Fair enough, but how often are we drinking wines so special that someone would want to fake them? And even when we are, a determined fraudster can fake the cork, too. So for the great majority of the time, the best advice is to put the cork aside, lift your glass, and let your nose and palate help you get on with the good part.

55 YOU DON'T EVEN NEED TO SIP

If you crave instant and unconditional gastronomic credibility—the kind of admiration normally reserved for lionized chefs—follow my lead. When a waiter presents you with the first taste of wine, swirl and sniff it, but refrain from sipping it, which is usually done to see if the wine is fresh or spoiled.

You can do this because most of taste is in fact smell. While the nose has the sensitivity to detect innumerable smells, our sense of taste is much more constrained, largely limited to a handful of flavors. As olfactory expert and author Rachel Herz has written, "Flavor is simply an aroma you can eat." So virtually everything you need to know to tell if a wine has spoiled—especially the wet newspaper aroma of cork taint or the Sherry-like or nutty aroma of oxidation (chapter 71)—comes from the preview you get from sniffing the wine. Taste, conversely, isn't as revealing and sometimes can mislead the mouth that hasn't yet adjusted to wine.

Savvy sommeliers are aware of the primacy of the sniff, so nosing the wine without sipping it will give them the impression that you are as much of a boss as the bearded Dos Equis man or his female equivalent. Your technique will also amuse your dining companions and give you an opportunity to gently inform them of the power of the olfactory sense in wine appreciation.

56 DON'T LET 'EM STRAND YOUR BOTTLE

There are certain bedeviling inevitabilities in restaurants. If you twice delay ordering, your server may disappear forever. If the server does not write down your order, he is probably going to get it wrong. And if he takes away your bottle, your glass will probably not be replenished when you need it.

On the last: Usually it starts innocently enough after your first glass is poured. "Would you like me to put that on ice?" asks the server graciously, and you answer in the affirmative. Or maybe the bottle is just whisked away. Either way: wish it bon voyage, because like the Rolling Stones album, it is heading for exile on Main Street. A top-off may or may not be poured when you need it, but the next pour—the critical lubrication for your main course—is as likely to show up on time as Charlie Sheen to an Eagle Scout jamboree.

What can you do if your waiter appears to be keeping your wine captive? Gently request it be left on the table. "We'd like to look at the label" is the pretext I will give to avoid seeming too dictatorial. If the wine needs to chill, request a cooling sleeve for the table or ask that a freestanding wine bucket be placed near your table. So be warned: placing your wine out of sight often jettisons it out of your server's mind.

57 ASK THEM TO SHOCK YOUR RED (AFTER A FIRST POUR)

If restaurants ever dared to offer the guarantee "Red served too warm? Dinner's on us," there would be a lot of free meals. So often the temperature of red wine gets forgotten about, even at wine-intensive restaurants, such that the red arrives at a relatively toasty room temperature of 72 to 75 degrees. Chilling a red makes it more refreshing, reduces your perception of its alcoholic heat, and focuses its flavors. Once you come to this realization, as many burgeoning oenophiles do, drinking reds with a bit of a chill becomes almost a necessity.

One solution is to add ice to your wine, which I will later explain is perfectly reasonable for everyday wine and especially if you have ordered it by the glass (chapter 64). But if it is a bottle that you want to enjoy throughout dinner, ask your waiter to chill it on ice for ten minutes. To keep things friendly, I usually make the request with the informal shorthand, "Would you give this bottle a shock on ice for ten minutes or so?"

I always ask the waiter to pour out a half glass of the yet-to-be-chilled red before it heads to ice. This tide-over pour is vital, because the only thing worse than a warm red is no red at all.

58 ANOTHER BOTTLE DOESN'T NECESSITATE A FRESH GLASS

Having a pristine glass placed before you for a different bottle of wine, as is often done in fine restaurants, is like turndown service in a hotel: a pleasure to have but by no means necessary. When my lips were barely wet with oenophilia, I assumed that a new bottle of wine always necessitated a new glass, like the next course of a meal gets its own plate.

What a relief it was to notice how relaxed many wine professionals are about the need for replacement glassware. Unless we are judging multiple wines at a trade competition, most of us are content to reuse the same glass, knowing that any lingering traces of the previous wine are not going to have a meaningful effect on the new wine. If there is any doubt, think about what happens at walk-around wine tastings: one glass suffices for what can be dozens of different types of wine, and nobody gets hurt. Of course, you always have the option of rinsing your glass with water. Though this can be slightly dilutive to the wine, a water rinse can be useful when making a considerable shift, such as from a sweet to a dry or a red to a white.

Another option is called "seasoning" or "priming" the glass, whereby one swirls a bit of the wine and then dumps it out. This avoids the risk of dilution, and when done before a first glass, it removes any musty odor from glasses stored in wooden cabinets. I do not normally bother with this so-called wine wash, unless I want to amuse my tablemates with the French translation for priming the glass, which is *"aviner le verre"* ("get the glass drunk").

59 PROTEST THE OVERZEALOUS POUR

It would be hard to state the case against aggressive wine pouring more potently than did the late writer and iconoclast Christopher Hitchens when he wrote on Slate.com in 2012, "Not only is it a breathtaking act of rudeness in itself, but it conveys a none-too-subtle and mercenary message: Hurry up and order another bottle." The restaurant wine pour may not be quite the "vile" act Hitchens cheekily describes, but its hurried application is a universal frustration. You should therefore have no compunction about telling your waiter to curb his or her enthusiasm and wait for you to signal for a refill. Of course, that hasty waiter isn't always out for the upsell; sometimes he or she is just looking to be helpful. Either way, the practice is so prevalent that it is up to the diner to be prepared to adjust the serving speed, or simply request to take control of the pour.

Overpouring isn't just about how often a waiter refills the glasses but also about how much those pours contain. Generally speaking, a restaurant's pour level correlates with the cluelessness of its wine program. So at a wine-savvy Danny Meyer restaurant, you are likely to get no more than one-third to one-half in your glass, which graciously allows for splash-free swirling and nosing of the wine. At the Applebee's in Tuskegee, it will probably be filled to the brim. This would qualify as generosity if the wine were being offered by the glass. But if the server is pouring from your bottle, it is unwieldy and often an indirect means of padding the bill. You have every right to request less in your glass.

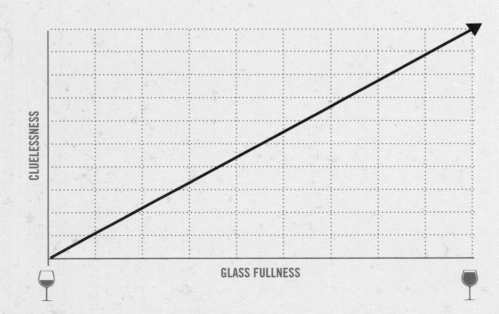

CLUELESSNESS

GLASS FULLNESS

60 PROTECT YOUR FINAL DROPS LIKE FORT KNOX

Last week, at a trendy Japanese restaurant, my girlfriend and I started our meal with some needlessly expensive edamame. Before long, only one fuzzy, chlorophyll-green squiggle remained, but the waiter suddenly pounced and whisked it away. I did not protest because it seemed petty to quibble over one lonely pod, but I cannot deny that my mouth was looking forward to that last warm and salty nibble.

The same happens with wine. In the name of turning over more tables or encouraging you to reorder more wine, some waiters prematurely pull away your close-to-empty bottle or glasses without even asking your permission.

Let's be clear: If there is just a smidgen left, it is your precious drop to enjoy. (Even if the glass is empty, its residue can be a pleasure to inhale, as we learned previously.) Not only is it perfectly reasonable to prize your last bit as you would a final bite of chocolate cake, but a restaurant truly invested in the art of hospitality will respect the sanctity of your last drop. If the server seizes it prematurely, feel free to ask for it back.

Many are unaware that in parts of Europe final drops get more respect. In France and Switzerland, they are known as *"les amours de la bouteille,"* and whoever gets to consume the last drop is supposed to be lucky in love. Sometimes the drinker will seal the deal by kissing the bottom of the bottle while invoking *"les amours."* Romantic as it is, the commitment-phobic should be aware that taking the last drop can also mean that you will marry within a year or that a baby girl will soon be on the way.

61 ONE TYPE OF GLASS IS ALL YOU NEED

If we had a secret camera that could peer into the dining rooms of the wineglass executives who perpetuate the notion that we need a wide array of glass shapes, I imagine that we would observe many of them contentedly making do with just one stem for all of their imbibing needs. Like high-fee financial advisers who quietly invest their own money in low-cost index funds, they do not follow their own advice.

Despite the fact that Riedel and other glassware purveyors decree that varietal-specific glasses can make a difference, I join many insiders in contending that the considerable expense of these glasses (and the heartache experienced when they inevitably shatter into glittering nonexistence) aren't worth the slight improvement they may make in the enjoyment of the wine.

To be sure, I prize my Kate Moss Champagne coupes (chapter 66) and the Victorian goblets hiding in my cupboards. But I did not acquire them with the assumption that they would directly improve a wine's taste—though the delicate, filigreed supermodel-inspired coupes do always manage to make the spirit soar. The truth is that I don't *need* any of these glasses, and I get to use them about as often as I would a crystal punch bowl or a fondue set.

Instead, follow my lead and think of glassware like you would a graham cracker: thin, big, and cheap. Your wineglass should be slender because you want to taste the wine—not the glass—with a wide bowl that holds at least twenty-two ounces so you have plenty of room to swirl and sniff your wine. Choose inexpensive glasses because glasses break as inevitably as earphones, smartphone screens, and the hearts of Chicago Cubs fans. Use that one glass type for your white, red, dessert, and sparkling wines, and reinvest your savings in a closet full of daily Prosecco.

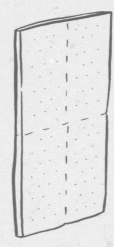

62 BUY ALL THE WINE TOOLS YOU NEED FOR $15

My penchant for useful wine gadgets knows no bounds. I love my Coravin, the mosquito-like needle that allows me to taste a wine without pulling its cork. My screw-and-prongs Durand corkscrew has extracted many an old, fragile cork. And nothing is more impressive than serving a big bottle from my Swiss-made VCANTER decanting cradle, a chrome-and-black crankable ramp that adorns my kitchen like a postmodern jewel box.

The sober truth, however, is that none of these gizmos, nor any other of the infinite number of wine tools on the market, are essential to appreciate even the finest wine. Like we should disregard those who urge the necessity of wine-specific glasses, we should dismiss those who say that the wine drinker needs to be outfitted with a range of expensive tools. In fact, it is fair to say that you need not invest more than $15 to have everything you need.

CORKSCREW:

Whether rabbit-style, wing-arm, self-pulling, or two-prong, there is a galaxy of cork extractors available. However, nothing beats the simple Waiter's Friend corkscrew for sheer ease of use, affordability, and portability. Look for ones with a Teflon-coated spiral, for easy drilling, and a little serrated blade to cut the foil off the bottleneck. Perfectly fine versions are widely available for $3 to $8.

PITCHER:

The only other mandatory tool is a decanting vessel, which is a fancy way to say you need a pouring container in the event you want to decant your wine to soften its tannins or remove its sediment (see chapter 67). But before you drop hundreds of dollars for one of the many fragile, curvy glass decanters available, be advised that a simple glass pitcher in your kitchen will suffice. In fact, I know a club of happy connoisseurs who are fine with using a Tupperware pitcher to decant their priceless bottles. With tongue firmly in cheek, they affectionately refer to their trusty vessel as the club crystal.

63 SERVE REDS COOLER, WHITES (POSSIBLY) WARMER

The temperature of wine is so vital that I stress the importance of chilling reds no fewer than three times in this book. Like the lighting of a room or the sauce of a dish, the temperature of wine has a dramatic influence on your perception of its taste.

Although it can seem counterintuitive to instill a chill into your reds, the advantages are many. Not only does it make the wine more refreshing, but it also brings out the acidity and makes the wine livelier in your mouth and more companionable with food. Chilling also tones down the hot, nose-in-the-snifter sensation you get from certain high-alcohol reds.

Commonly chilled reds are gulpable, leaner reds, such as Beaujolais and lighter versions of Pinot Noir, but I like to make sure all of my reds are at least cool. Some tasters prefer not to chill heavy reds because it can deaden some of the nuance and accentuate tannic bitterness.

The risk of numbing flavor is also the reason some advise against serving white wine too cold. While I agree in the case of a special occasion white—say a pricey Napa Chardonnay or Meursault from France—I prefer that most whites, and almost all of my bubbly and dessert wine, arrive quite cold. Not only are they more refreshing and food-flatteringly crisp this way, but the wine is going to warm up a bit anyway, so it is better to err on the side of coolness and appreciate its subtleties as they blossom in the glass. And if you find that it is too cold out of the gate for your taste, you can always warm up your glass by cupping both hands around it, a pro maneuver that will demonstrate your savoir faire.

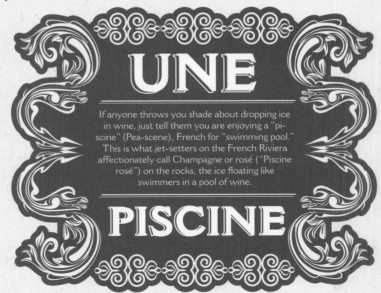

UNE PISCINE

If anyone throws you shade about dropping ice in wine, just tell them you are enjoying a "piscine" (Pea-scene), French for "swimming pool." This is what jet-setters on the French Riviera affectionately call Champagne or rosé ("Piscine rosé") on the rocks, the ice floating like swimmers in a pool of wine.

64 GO AHEAD, ADD ICE

Drop ice into your wine and some will react as if you have toted a Chihuahua to the opera. What they don't realize, however, is that many of wine's leading lights have no qualms about cooling off their wine with ice, especially if it is a simple, everyday wine whose taste you do not have to worry about diluting. Cooling down wine not only makes it taste more refreshing, it also focuses its flavors and tones down your perception of the wine's alcoholic heat.

I especially like using ice in restaurants when a wine is served too warm, as is commonly the case. *The Wall Street Journal* has reported that the late wine writer Alexis Bespaloff had a "four-second rule" in which he would drop a cube in his glass, swirl it around for four seconds, and then remove it. Experiencing no dilution anxiety myself, I like to leave the cube swimming for a good twenty to thirty seconds, and even longer for white wine; sometimes I just let the ice stay and dissolve its way into oblivion. Whichever way you do it, just be sure to give your waiter a cheeky wink while you are doing it.

If you are still hesitant about whether it is acceptable to add ice to wine, it is a little-known fact that America's fine-wine pioneer, the late Robert Mondavi, would sometimes drink his wine on the rocks. Famously relaxed and unpretentious about wine, the Californian vintner would think nothing of dropping a cube into a glass of his Cabernet Sauvignon on a warm summer evening.

If you still cannot bring yourself to do it, know that at home there are two ingenious ways to lower a wine's temperature. The first is to keep a handful of grapes frozen in your freezer and drop in a few whenever you need to cool down your wine. The other is to freeze an ice tray with white wine and plop in a cube or two whenever you feel the zeal to get cool.

65 FOUR SECRET STEPS TO SUPERCHARGE AN ICE BUCKET

What can be more straightforward than chilling your wine in an ice bucket? Simply locate a deep bucket, add some cubes, insert the wine, and wait fifteen minutes.

Slow down, my wayward tendril, we can make this process cooler, faster, and more rewarding. I have four easy, neglected steps to forever enhance your chilling prowess:

1 USE LESS ICE. YOU NEED ONLY FILL A THIRD OF THE BUCKET WITH ICE BECAUSE YOU will also be adding water, as described next.

2 ADD WATER. THIS OFT-NEGLECTED STEP IS DONE TO CREATE AN ICE BATH THAT will submerge the bottle up to its neck. The water fills the air pockets between the cubes and pulls heat away from the wine faster than the ice alone. Mixing water with ice also makes it much easier to maneuver the wine in and out of the ice bucket.

3 ADD SALT. IF POSSIBLE, ADD A FEW FISTFULS OF SALT TO THE MIX. SALT LOWERS the freezing temperature of water, not unlike the salt used to melt icy winter roads.

4 SPIN THE BOTTLE. ADD YOUR BOTTLE AND GENTLY SPIN IT AT FIRST AND AFTER A few minutes to ensure that all of the wine is exposed to the ice bath.

In five minutes your reds will be cool, and in twice that time, your whites, bubbly, and dessert wine, fully chilled.

66 FAVOR A FULL-FIGURED GLASS FOR CHAMPAGNE

As soon as I heard that Kate Moss had authorized a limited-edition Champagne glass molded on her breasts, I knew ordering a set was a drop-everything glassware emergency. Arriving from London encased in a hunter green box, they proved themselves to be odes to glamorous plentitude, wide and shallow and finely etched. This would not be the first time bubbly met the bosom: the saucer-shaped glass—or coupe (pronounced coo-pay)—was the Champagne vessel of choice early in the twentieth century, its comely shape for years mistakenly attributed to the décolletage of Marie Antoinette.

As wine pros became more concerned with preserving Champagne's effervescence and showcasing its chimney of bubbles, the thin, narrow flute became the dominant glass for bubbles. But about a decade ago, experts began favoring a return to a fuller-figured glass—not necessarily coupe-wide, mind you, but at least with the circumference of a white wineglass, or even, for some like me, the generosity of an all-purpose wineglass. Compared to the tapered flute, a standard wineglass affords more surface area to swirl and sniff while obviating the need for special glassware. While your bubbles will indeed dissipate faster, you will not notice it if you drink with sufficient gusto.

So even though flutes are still common on some tables and shelves, you should not hesitate in using a standard wineglass for your sparklers. When the occasion calls for it, I also advise you to keep a stash of coupes on hand, even better if they channel the allure of a supermodel. Like the gliding, in-through-the-back-door Copacabana scene in *Goodfellas*, the right coupe at the right time does everything but deliver you to a ringside table at the Copa.

"A SHOWER OF BRIGHT

INVERTED RAIN"

ENGLISH WRITER MARTIN ARMSTRONG
(1882—1974) DESCRIBING
CHAMPAGNE

67 DECANTING IS EASY AND NOT JUST FOR REDS

So much in food and wine is cloaked by words. People say maître d' when they mean host. An hors d'oeuvre is simply a small snack. And decanting, which sounds like an involved, almost alchemical process that requires specialized equipment and serious expense, means to pour wine into a pitcher, or even a flower vase or large mason jar, to let it air out.

Decanting is often performed to remove sediment that tends to form in an older red wine. You slowly pour the wine into a decanter (i.e., any large container), stopping when you see the sediment, or harmless clumpy deposits, once they float into the bottle neck. In this case, you are simply decanting to separate the wine from its age-related sediment; you are removing junk from the wine's trunk, so to speak.

The other classic reason for decanting is to soften an astringent, gum-drying wine by exposing it to more oxygen. It is often done with a big, rich red that has ample tannic bitterness, pouring it into a decanter and letting it breathe there for one to three hours or more. The decanter should be broad brimmed to allow the largest possible surface area of wine to aerate. For that extra-puckery Barolo or Cabernet, some enthusiasts will use two decanters to "double decant," pouring the wine back and forth for a few minutes to accelerate aeration. Either way, note that I wrote the word "aeration," not "transformation," since no amount of exposure of oxygen will turn a tannic bruiser into a cooing sweetheart.

That said, there is no downside to decanting, except in the rare case of very old wines whose final fragile flavors might be decimated by the extra oxygen. Decanting is also preferable to the expense and unpredictable results of a wine aerator (chapter 67).

Though usually the province of sturdy, full-bodied reds, it can be worth decanting white wines occasionally. It is fascinating to notice how a white changes after thirty to sixty minutes in a decanter. Often its nose is better for it, becoming more expressive or, in rare cases, shedding the struck-match, sulfurous smell that occasionally afflicts wine when it is first opened. In the unusual case of superdry, piercingly acidic whites wines like France's Savennières, some experts say that decanting is needed to make it more approachable.

Whether red or white, a final reason to decant is for the purposes of ritual and, to me, a certain feeling of dominion over your wine. Pouring wine into a glass vessel edges it out of the realm of the commercial and closer to something that is truly yours, like removing the logo from your favorite pair of jeans. Placing wine into a decanter makes it *your* personal elixir, the first of many that you should share with friends.

68 AVOID PRICEY AERATORS

Like buttons at crosswalks or the ones meant to close an elevator's door, wine aerators—those funnels or pourers that mix wine with air—are of questionable utility and seem to exist to give the user something to do. And unlike the first two examples, wine aerators have the additional disadvantage of putting you through the motions at considerable expense.

This is not to say that wine aerators have no effect on wine. Aerators such as Vinturi and Vintorio are designed to accelerate the process of decanting discussed previously. The hope is that your wine will taste softer, less bitter, and overall more delicious. After countless blind tastings with major aerators over the years, I can verify that the wine often tastes different from one poured directly from a newly opened bottle—but it is not always for the better. Sometimes the wine softens pleasingly, but other times it loses flavor, making the wine taste less bright and defined. (If you really want to short circuit the process of decanting, you can follow culinary mad scientist Nathan Myhrvold's lead and whiz your wine on high speed in a blender for a minute; like using an aerators, such "hyperdecanting" does indeed change the wine, but for me it faded the flavors and added some froth that did not subside.)

That is why my recommendation on a wine aerator is—in the snappy phraseology of an Australian friend—to "give it a miss." You are better off letting your wine sit for an hour in a simple, wide-rimmed container than dealing with the uncertainty and cost of an aerator. If you can't wait, pour yourself a tide-over glass.

The impulse to accessorize a passion is understandable; the birder longs for optically advanced binoculars; the speed junkie needs that next-generation radar detector. Wine enthusiasts, however, would be better served by forgoing an aerator in favor of something that always work, such as that extra bottle of wine and a simple jar in which to aerate it.

ANNÉE 2006   P. 140

FLAWS

NO. 0008

Mise en Bouteille au Domaine

13% ALC. BY VOL   PRODUCT OF NEW YORK   750 ML

69 "CORKED" WINE IS ENEMY NUMBER ONE, BUT IT ISN'T ALWAYS OBVIOUS

Whether at a restaurant or around your kitchen table, you should always take a moment to smell your wine to see if it is in good condition. Ask a casual drinker what spoiled wine smells like, and they will probably say "vinegar." Who hasn't inhaled the pungent, sour, and nutty aroma of wine you forgot to throw away? This, of course, is the sign your wine has oxidized—that is, it has been exposed to excessive amounts of oxygen.

The more common wine fault to look for, however, is the mildewy smell of wet newspaper, a basement floor, or, as I like to say, a waterlogged Toyota Corolla. This dank smell indicates that the wine is "corked," or afflicted with a chemical that comes from a tainted cork or, less often, contamination on the production line at the winery. Along with the moldy smell, the wine itself will often taste flat and flavorless. This can happen to wine of any quality, so don't just blame your sister's bottle of 7-Eleven's finest. In my experience, about 5 percent of wine suffers from cork taint.

Identifying cork taint is not like a trigonometry problem or a pregnancy test: The answer is not always clear-cut. When a wine exudes a fiercely dank cardboard-y smell, of course, you know you have a corked wine. But cork taint sometimes operates less conspicuously.

It is better to think of cork taint as a sliding scale, one in which there is sometimes only a whiff of basement-y stench. And, frustratingly, sometimes a corked wine is even harder to detect and only manifests itself in wine that is surprisingly devoid of aromas and flavor. Such subtlety stumps even experienced palates. When faced with the corked question, I will look for a second opinion and pass the glass to a tablemate or two, asking them if the wine seems off. In a restaurant, I will ask my server for confirmation, too, rather than rejecting the wine with Simon Cowellian cocksurety. The process becomes less confrontational when you give your server some ownership over the process, inviting him to smell and taste the wine, or take the bottle back to the sommelier or bartender to do so.

In certain instances, however, it is better to hold your fire. When I was recently at a celebratory dinner with a table full of casual drinkers, the waiter poured us a Cabernet Sauvignon that seemed corked. I thought about saying something until I observed that no one else seemed bothered by this corky cuvée. Corked wine will not hurt you, so why should I interrupt their merriment with the doleful notes of a Debbie Downer trombone? I quietly choked down a glass, happy to let ignorance be bliss.

CORK TAINT: A CONTINUUM

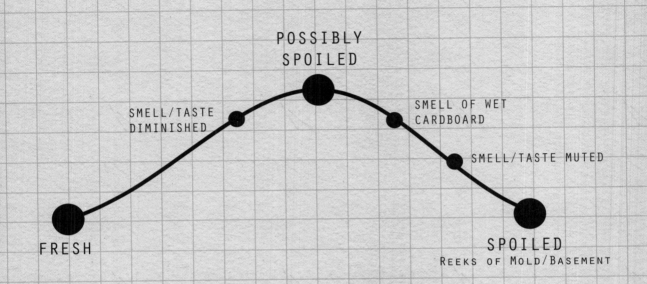

POSSIBLY
SPOILED

SMELL/TASTE
DIMINISHED

SMELL OF WET
CARDBOARD

SMELL/TASTE MUTED

FRESH

SPOILED
REEKS OF MOLD/BASEMENT

OTHER FLAWS

OTHER WORRISOME FLAWS ARE SIGNALED BY A WHIFF OF:

- PRUNES, STEWED FRUIT: WINE IS "COOKED," FROM EXPOSURE TO EXCESSIVE HEAT
- NUTTY, SHERRY-LIKE: WINE IS "OXIDIZED," FROM EXPOSURE TO EXCESSIVE OXYGEN
- BAND-AIDS, UNPLEASANT BARNYARD: WINE IS "BRETTY," FROM EXCESSIVE AMOUNTS OF THE YEAST BRETTANOMYCES)
- BURNT MATCHES/ROTTEN EGGS: SULFUR-RELATED FLAW.

ENEMY NUMBER ONE, HOWEVER, REMAINS THE MUSTY, MOLDY, SPIRIT-SLAYING STENCH OF CORK TAINT.

70 EMBRACE CORKED WINE

Once you happen upon a wine that is corked—I mean hurricane-savaged basement, wrestling-shoes-in-a-locker corked—fight the urge to whisk it away as if it were a fly in your soup. Counterintuitively, consider keeping it on the table, or have your server do so, because it is one of wine's unsung learning opportunities.

This is because knowing when a wine is corked is fundamental to wine appreciation, so much so that it is largely why we are asked to test the wine we order in restaurants. As I explain in chapter 69, however, its identification can be frustratingly elusive to the uninitiated, in part because a wine can be only *partially* corked and also one afflicted with cork taint typically gets removed from the table so quickly that other diners do not get a chance to inhale its moldy charms for themselves.

So if you have a corked wine in your midst, treat it as if you have captured a rare Sierra Nevada red fox: approach with care, but take the time to get to know it. Pass a glass of it around your table for others to smell it; they may cringe at its malodorousness at first but will later appreciate that someone has *finally* shown them exactly what to smell for in judging cork taint. In fact, when I come across an obviously corked wine at my seminars, as happens occasionally, I experience not disappointment but elation, because passing it through the audience offers an olfactory lesson of a lifetime.

71 SOME FLAWS CAN BE OVERLOOKED

My beautiful friend is every regular guy's dream: She seeks not square-jawed Adonises but happily accepts prominent paunches, crooked noses, and protruding ears. Jowls of a scowling Nixon? Raccoon eyes of actor Vincent Schiavelli? Bone structure of Lyle Lovett? She can handle all of it, as long as the man treats her well and makes her laugh.

So it is with wine: some flaws are not fatal and can be overlooked if the underlying wine tastes good. Take, for example, bits of cork in a wine. They don't affect a wine's flavor and can be strained away with a coffee filter or kitchen strainer if needed. What about the white, rock salt–like crystals occasionally lurking in wine or on the end of the cork? No stress: these are just tartar crystals—a harmless, tasteless result of wine being stored at an unusually cold temperature.

How about the seemingly scary sight of a pushed-up cork or sticky streaks on the bottle's neck? This happens when a bottle has been exposed to excessive heat. In some cases, the wine will indeed be "cooked," that is, afflicted with disappointingly flat or stewed flavors, but in other cases it will be perfectly fine. Taste it and find out.

What if a wine has an unexpectedly Sherry-like character? That is a sign of oxidization, likely because of a faulty cork seal but occasionally because the winemaker intended the wine to have that style. So long as it doesn't overwhelm the other elements in the wine, it can be yours to enjoy.

Even the inglorious smell of horse manure doesn't necessarily invalidate wine's drinkability. As previously covered, that barnyard-y aroma is often from the yeast, Brettanomyces, which can occur at several stages of wine production. When it comes in small doses, some drinkers are quite fond of it, viewing Brett as a savory, funky dimension in the wine.

72 BROKEN CORKS ARE MORE BARK THAN BITE

Have you experienced BCP? No, it's not one of those acronyms that drug companies are trying to sell you a medicine for, although its impact does read like a rambling recitation of side effects, including sweaty palms, shaking, anxiety, and loss of appetite.

I'm talking about broken cork panic, an affliction that most of us have experienced when pulling out a cork. It takes hold when the cork snaps in two, causing you and your guests to fret that something is wrong with the wine. This concern, happily enough, is largely unjustified. Broken corks happen more often than people realize, occurring with regularity in bottles both simple and sublime.

The key is to realize that cork breakage is often more about the corkscrew, like when the screw is too dull or the person using it is, and we forget to maneuver the screw deep enough into the cork.

The first solution is to insert the screw into the remaining cork, going in at an angle, and to try to use the edge of the inside of the bottle as an anchor. The trick here is to screw in diagonally and slowly lever out the cork piece.

If the remaining cork breaks up in the bottle, find a mesh strainer and simply pour the wine through it, filtering out the pieces of cork into a decanter underneath the strainer. Alternatively, strain the wine through a coffee filter or cheesecloth. If you don't get every piece, no need for BCP: cork fragments, or a pushed-in cork, do not adversely affect the taste of the wine.

To be sure, a crumbly cork can occasionally indicate that the bottle seal was compromised and the wine has become oxidized. But in most cases, a broken cork is, literally and figuratively, more bark than bite.

“Part

Stor

Vin

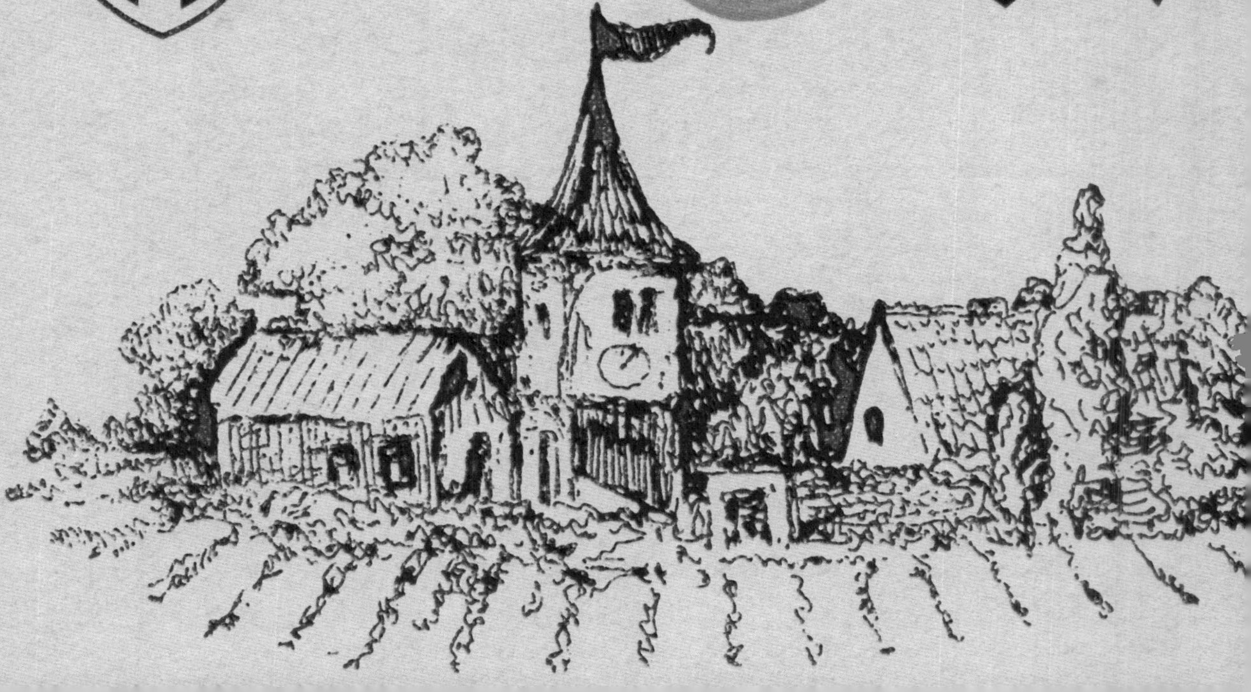

"Seven"

age &

tage

APPELLATION CHABLIS
GRAND CRU CONTRÔLÉE

13% ALC./VOL

73 LEFTOVER WINE LASTS LONGER THAN YOU THINK

While I don't believe in wine rules, if I had to issue one myself, it would be this: thou shall leave no leftover wine. Wine is usually best when it is fresh from the bottle and in plentiful portions, shared with others or with a willing boeuf bourguignon.

Alas, it's not always practical to polish off your bottle, and this is where the confusion starts: many consumers have the impression that wine is primed to wilt after a day or two. Over the years, I have come to discover that opened wines are more durable than commonly thought. While that delicate, aged red Burgundy may not have more than a day or two until its flavors go flat, I find that many wines will last for a week if properly stored. In particular, hardy reds—such as tannic, astringent renditions of Cabernet Sauvignon and Barolo—can actually get better for a day or two with the extra air that comes from having been opened. High-acid whites—especially the simple, everyday type—can stay drinkable for over a week.

Just make sure to recork opened bottles and store them, even the reds, in the refrigerator, as the coldness slows biological deterioration. All the better if the wine has a screw cap—the airtight seal will contribute to its staying power. If you feel like making the effort, use a rubber Vacu Vin saver or similar device to pump out excess air from the bottle, or transfer the wine to a smaller bottle (even a plasic water bottle) to prolong its life.

What many people do not know is that you can even treat your unused wine like Thanksgiving leftovers and send it straight to the freezer, which is an especially useful technique in the common case of large format bottles that do not get finished. The wine fits best in my freezer in a large, screw-capped water bottle, where it will remain fresh for many months. When you're ready to drink it, give it a few hours to thaw or transfer it to your refrigerator to thaw overnight. Don't fret if you see a few crystals floating in the wine: they are harmless by-product of the coldness and a small price to pay for preserving wine that you want to experience again.

74 THINK TWICE BEFORE AGING THAT WINE

I t ages like fine wine" is the common refrain that has misled generations of wine drinkers to believe that fine wine necessarily gets better with years in the bottle.

The truth is that only about 2 percent of the world's wine actually becomes more interesting and complex with age. Most wine produced today is made for immediate drinking—perfectly tasty at release and not able to bring anything more to the table later on. Some wines can remain drinkable for several years but do not actually transform into something better with bottle age. The tiny subset of bottles that actually improves tend to have noticeable levels of tannin and acidity that gradually diminish over the years, leaving a greater range of aromas and flavors in their wake. After ten years or more, a successfully aged wine will show intriguing aromas, such as mushrooms, leather, and earth.

Besides having considerable tannin and acidity, as well as sufficient flavor intensity—the combination of which is deemed "structure" in winespeak—how do you know if your wine is one of the minuscule group that is age-worthy? Certain grapes have a track record for ageability, such as tannic, thick-skinned Cabernet or Nebbiolo. A wine's vintage year (chapter 77) can also tip you off to its potential for aging, as well as its reproducer's reputation for making age-worthy wine. Reviews in online databases such as CellarTracker.com and WineSpectator.com and in apps like Delectable are also useful in determining which bottles are best for socking away, or "laying down" in wine parlance.

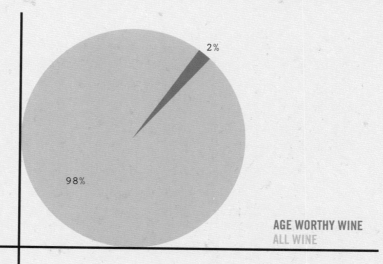

2%

98%

AGE WORTHY WINE
ALL WINE

75 SOME WHITES GET BETTER WITH AGE

What wine enthusiast has not dreamed of having his or her own stately stone cellar, its cobweb-encrusted bottles of red wine making their slow and steady journey to maturity?

But why red wine? We traditionally think of age-worthy wine as red because wine of that color is fermented with the grapes' skins and thus has the astringency—i.e., the tannins—that gradually diminishes and reveals intriguing aromas and flavors.

What is not commonly known is that tannins are not the only element that can make a wine become more interesting with age. Acidity is also a factor in the ageability of wine, and the primary reason whites, albeit a microscopically small group of them, can also improve with age despite having little or no tannin.

High-acid whites such as certain Rieslings, Chenin Blanc from the Loire Valley, and white Burgundy can transform into something special after ten years or more. A daring sommelier once showed me that even the relatively simple charms of Muscadet (chapter 99) can transcend their initial character with some bottle age. The fruit flavors of young wine are replaced by intriguing hints of honeysuckle, nuts, or even the eyebrow-raising scent of gasoline (see chapter 19). While time typically softens their acidity, the best of these aged whites retain a tongue-tingling crispness. If any doubt remains about the appeal of aged whites, know that many of my insider friends name not a red but a well-aged white as their all-time favorite wine.

> *"This Burgundy seemed to me, then, serene and triumphant, a reminder that the world was an older and better place . . ."*
> —*Evelyn Waugh, Brideshead Revisited (1945)*

76 FOREPLAY WITH AGED WINE CAN BE BETTER THAN THE REAL THING

Mature wine for me is a tale of two tastes: many of the best wines I have tasted were aged, yet in truth, many of the worst ones came from years in the cellar, too. As we previously covered, only a tiny fraction of wine actually improves with age. But even if you have one of those, it does not mean it is going to taste delicious.

This is because aged wine is always a guessing game, no matter how experienced or careful you are. Improper storage, such as exposure to excessive heat, can turn a great wine into a bland zombie. Or maybe that bottle of fine old Burgundy was counterfeited, as is increasingly common with the world's great ageable wines. Even a properly stored, authentic bottle can disappoint if one waits too long to drink it, missing the wine's so-called drinking window. And sometimes you can get the timing right but still not like how that particular wine has evolved—too much earth, excessively leathery, or just not enough *there* there.

Here is the secret: the more pleasurable part of experiencing mature wine is often in the foreplay rather than the actual act. It is found in the acquisition of the bottle or the friends who are willing to kindly share it with you. It resides in the anticipatory thrill of sampling something rare and expensive. It lies in the nostalgia of thinking back to what life was like in the vintage year you are drinking, and the merriment and mischief that transpired then.

RENOWNED WINE EXPERT AND AUCTIONEER

Dennis Foley, who has tasted more great wine that any wine pro I know, revealed to me an unconventional way of bringing an over-the-hill wine back to drinkability. For over-the-hill vintages of wine such as Burgundy and Port, he unapologetically adds a bit of fresh wine young wine of the same type. The same goes for decades-old Champagne that has lost its effervesce and acidity; he resuscitates it by splashing an entry-level Champagne such as Moet & Chandon's "White Star."

77 DITCH THE VINTAGE CHART

With the concern most of us feel about making the wrong wine decision, it is understandable that we long for the equivalent of a divining rod to the good bottles. Enter the vintage chart, that seemingly important document that rates the weather conditions from a region in a particular year. A good vintage is one in which the grapes get fully ripe, which typically happens in the presence of consistently dry, sunny days and cool nights; a lesser vintage is one dogged by frost or rain or other conditions that impair ripeness and thus wine quality.

While some publications and experts still create the impression that a vintage chart can crack the code of wine purchasing like a hacker in a hoodie, the reality is that it is largely unnecessary these days. Not only is this because

GO

While it is wise to avoid obsessing over vintage charts, the opportunity to observe "vintage variation"—or how one particular wine changes through the years—is one of oenophilia's great joys. This is why the so-called "vertical tastings" offered at restaurants and wine festivals can be worth their cost, affording you the chance to experience how the same wine fared across years of differing precipitation, temperature, and other grape-influencing factors.

VERTICAL

much of the wine we consume comes from regions that are dependably sunny, including so-called New World places such as California and Australia, and much of Spain, but because today a winemaker's skill coupled with technology can largely outsmart a disappointing vintage. Choosing a good producer is therefore much more important than worrying about the vintage.

This is not to say that vintage year doesn't matter. It is the reason your favorite wine, even those from warmer climates, will never be exactly the same in subsequent vintages. In the case of special wines from meteorologically challenged, cool-climate areas like Bordeaux, Burgundy, and northern Italy, vintage year can have even more variation. Vintage considerations are especially important in the case of the relatively tiny amount of age-worthy, auction-grade wines whose prices are often keyed to the hype surrounding a particular vintage year. Even then, however, there is no need to memorize vintage scores or keep a chart in your wallet; all of the information you need is a mere Google search away.

That Monumental Vintage

The "Vintage of the Century" announced by certain wineries and shops often amounts to hyperbole designed to play on the consumer's fear of missing out. Many enthusiasts, especially newer ones unfamiliar with the rhythms of the industry, do not realize that extraordinary, must-have vintages are announced every few years. The wonderful thing about wine is that there is always another vintage coming. Yet to many profiting from the sale of wine, as an old Bordeaux saying goes, "The best vintage is the one they are currently selling."

May Not Be So

EIGHT

sing

78 WINE'S SWEET SPOT IS $15 TO $25

Although we have established that price is not necessarily proportionate to deliciousness, there is nevertheless a range in which you are likely to get the most pleasure relative to the dollars you spend. Most experts agree that this sweet spot spans from $15 to $25.

Hold on, I hear you say. You've had perfectly pleasing bottles that rang up for less than $15. Yes, and so have I. What I mean, however, is that below $15—and especially below $10—it becomes increasingly difficult to find memorable cuvées, ones that will delight you with seductive aromas and flavors and texture. Serviceable, solid picnic-level wines are abundant beneath the sweet spot; seriously made bottles, ones that convey a sense of where they are from, with qualities special enough to remember, are not.

What about the bottles above $25, an area I myself flirt with on occasion. To be sure, the finest, most coveted wine—including most of the truly transcendent juice that has passed my lips—originates from the finest vineyards and has been handled by an expert team. Making wine of this caliber is not an inexpensive endeavor. But in most cases, once you hurdle $25 or $30, the price decreasingly reflects the costs of production and is due more to scarcity and to what the market is willing to bear.

So the lesson is clear: if you are willing to pay at least $15 for a bottle, it becomes markedly easier to find wines that stand out for specialness. Think of it like a hamburger: while a mass-market chain can deliver a perfectly palatable, if unremarkable, meal, spending just a bit more for a local favorite is more likely to deliver a memorable meal. At the same time, paying three times as much for that super-trendy, foie gras–stuffed burger, however exciting, is less about the inherent quality of the food and more about the excitement of the experience.

79 SOME WINES REQUIRE A BIT MORE CASH

Some wines (e.g., Vinho Verde) are always inexpensive, while others (e.g., red Burgundy) are infamously costly. There are, however, several types that run the gamut of pricing such that it is not always clear when it's safe to purchase bottles at the lower end or when you need to spend a bit more for quality.

Consider Domaines Ott and a handful of other luxury rosés. You can spend extra for them, but generally speaking, that additional expenditure doesn't bring dramatically more nuance or flavor than what you will get from most $15 rosés. (If you want to pass me your bottle, however, I shall glug it down with appreciative zeal.) Similarly, it may not be worth spending extra for wine types such as American sparkling wine, whites from Greece, and Portuguese reds, because their basic versions tend to be reliably satisfying. To proffer a sartorial analogy: why buy the super-luxury socks when many modest ones ably get the job done?

Other kinds of wine are more like sushi: the low end is fraught with peril and opening your wallet slightly wider can improve your experience markedly. Pinot Noir is a perfect example. The extra handling required to grow this finicky grape almost always necessitates forking over $25 or more at retail to avoid an under-ripe dullard. Duds, of course, exist at every price level, but Pinot Noir tends to show especially poorly at its least expensive, as do Chianti, Merlot, and Valpolicella. While you'll search far and wide for good ones below $10, a willingness to pay twice that or a bit more can bring you a world of difference in quality.

80 SOME PRODUCERS CREATE THE ILLUSION OF SCARCITY

When the seventeenth century French courtesan Ninon de L'Enclos declared, "Love never dies of starvation, but often of indigestion," she had no idea that she was also explaining a major ingredient in the success of some wines today. Actually, it is the idea's inverse that underpins the allure of certain wines: love can be created by starvation.

The aura of scarcity pervades so much of wine. Think of all the wines labeled "Reserve" whether they deserve it or not, and the prevalence of "prestige" and other words that create the impression of limited supply and heightened quality. They are like an airline's "elite" status: if they have to call themselves that, they are probably anything but.

Then there is some wineries' use of mailing lists, which is their equivalent of a club's velvet rope. Tell people they can't come in and they'll break down your door to get inside. Some regions are indeed self-limited by geographical constraints. The entire length of Burgundy's prime zone, for example, is only thirty miles long; its relative paucity of vineyard land is the driver in why wine from that region is so staggeringly expensive, regardless of whether a bottle of Burgundy is memorably luscious or essentially a bottle of flavored acid water.

Then there are wineries that carefully manage their scarcity, purposefully playing hard to get. Producers of Napa cult Cabernet, faced now with less demand than they enjoyed a generation ago, are allegedly storing excess bottles in warehouses. They do this while telling the world that their supplies are completely sold out. It is reminiscent of the diamond trade's tendency to stockpile diamonds to maintain their high cost, while announcing to the marketplace that shortages are soon to come. As New York restaurateur Joe Bastianich wrote in his revealing book *Restaurant Man,* the golden rule in winemaking is that "you always want to make six bottles short of what your distributor asks you for."

The most famous example of a wine company creating the impression of scarcity is Moët & Chandon's Dom Pérignon. Dom Pérignon burnishes its rarefied reputation by sponsoring top art festivals, polo tournaments, and Formula One teams, as well as doing label collaborations with the world's most expensive artists, such as Jeff Koons and Andy Warhol's estate. At the same time, although the company guards its production figures, several media outlets have estimated that Moët actually produces millions of bottles of Dom Pérignon each vintage. If that amount seems far-fetched given Dom Pérignon's heady reputation, consider that the largest retail purveyor of Dom Pérignon is a source far from manicured greens of polo fields: Costco Wholesale.

81 LOVE THY SCREW CAP

If anything should convince you of my position on screw caps, consider the stated location on my Twitter profile: "Wherever corks pop and caps snap." I give equal status to corks and twist-offs because both are perfectly acceptable bottle closures. A generation ago, the thought of packaging wine like soda pop would have prompted connoisseurs to raise their corkscrews in a vampire cross, the humble screw cap a surefire indicator of inferior wine.

These days quality wine is often packaged with screw caps, not only making the wine easier to open but also mostly protecting it from cork taint, the aforementioned moldy, basement-floor smell that experts estimate affect at least 5 percent of all cork-enclosed bottles. (Surprisingly, a screw-capped wine can still be afflicted with cork taint because the chemical that causes it can also infiltrate a winery's production line. But in most cases, cork is still the culprit.) Some topflight wineries close most or all of their wines with a screw cap, especially in New Zealand, Australia, and other countries unfettered by centuries of wine tradition.

Still concerned that the inglorious snap of a screw cap will undermine a wine's sophisticated aura? When first impressions count, such as a date or key business meeting, simply drape a towel over the neck of the bottle and pull the cap away inside the towel. Better yet, open the bottle in another room, pour the wine into a glass decanter, and your guests will never know that they are drinking wine opened with a humble crack.

"SPECIAL"

Glorious will be the day when a Public Enemy fan remixes the group's classic "Don't Believe the Hype" using the words on wine labels that have no legal definition. These include "Reserve" (seemingly an estate's finer wine), "Old Vines" (wine from decades-old, supposedly more flavorful grapes), and "hand-picked" grapes (presumably an indicator of better handling than those that are machine harvested). Often these words accurately reflect higher quality, but because they are unregulated in the United States, they are sometimes nothing more than empty copy.

MAY BE ANYTHING BUT

THE
WINE STORE

NO. <u>0009</u>

Mise en Bouteille au Domaine

13% ALC. BY VOL   **PRODUCT OF NEW YORK**   750 ML

82 START WITH A DIAGNOSTIC CASE

The best wine buying advice I ever received came not from a wine connoisseur but from a professional musician on a limited budget. His method is to go to a wine shop that he trusts and ask them to put together a mixed case of a particular category of wine, be it a region (e.g., Rhône Valley), subregion (e.g., Gigondas), or a grape (e.g., Syrah). He will specify a price per bottle limit and leave the store with what I call a diagnostic case. It is his wise way of drinking with a purpose.

Actually, there are several purposes. The first is monetary, as most stores offer a 10 to 20 percent discount for purchasing by the case. The next is determining whether there is a wine that is compelling enough to order additional cases to have on hand as a "house wine." He and his wife will open a bottle with dinner over the next few weeks, or he'll invite over a group of friends to enjoy some or all of the bottles. Either way, they will keep track of the favorite bottles with the goal of finding one or two standouts.

The final benefit of the diagnostic case is that it introduces him or, equally as important, reintroduces him to a particular wine category. I always tell my seminar attendees that spending time focusing solely on one particular type—say, Santa Barbara Chardonnay or reds from southern Italy—is the most effective way of deepening your familiarity with it. It teaches you the style variations within that type—such as the difference between the more grassy, acidic Sauvignon Blanc from New Zealand and the Loire versus the often tamer versions from Bordeaux and California. Think of it as investment in twelve well-priced opportunities to fall in love with a particular category and a particular style therein.

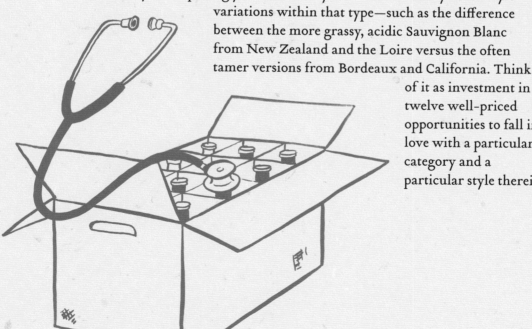

83 DON'T LIMIT YOUR BUYING TO ONE TYPE OF RETAILER

After my first book, *Oldman's Guide to Outsmarting Wine,* came out, a major independent wine shop in New York invited me to do a book signing. But when they noticed I had recommended Costco in the book, the general manager cancelled the signing. Puzzled, I inquired about the abrupt turnaround.

"You mentioned Costco," he said in a wounded tone, as if I had bedded their mortal enemy. "But you are a legendary Park Avenue merchant," I pointed out, "and Costco is a discount warehouse whose closest location is forty miles away." His only answer was an exasperated sigh as if to say, "But they are still a major threat to us."

This was my illuminating introduction to the sharp elbows of wine retailing, where long-established merchants can be threatened by a book's mere mention of a noncompetitor. What it said to me was that big-box retailers have advantages that even a long-established, ultra-confident business cannot match. The takeaway is that we consumers should not confine our purchases to one type of store, but should make use of all them for their respective strengths, detailed here:

INDEPENDENT SHOP:

The best way to discover smaller producers and offbeat categories. Quality merchants are happy to provide knowledgeable guidance, so find yourself a "wine spouse" (chapter 87). Prices tend to be somewhat higher to cover the personal attention given to customers. Many have in-store tastings so that you can sample before you buy. Some independents specialize in specific regions, such as Burgundy, California, or Spain.

BIG-BOX CHAINS, DISCOUNT RETAILERS, GROCERY STORES:

Compelling prices are their raison d'etre, though usually at the expense of personal attention, so they are best when you already know what you want. Grocery stores (in states that allow such alcohol sales) offer the convenience of buying wine while you shop for food. The selection tends to focus on unpretentious, large volume wines made to consume soon after purchase, although Costco will sometimes stock surprisingly high-end wine.

WEBSITES AND APPS:
A godsend for around-the-clock comparison shopping and searches of large swathes of inventory, especially that which would never fit on the shelves of a physical store. Some cater to connoisseur-focused categories such as auction-grade wine, Champagne, and Madeira. Drawbacks include delivery costs and shipping issues depending on state. You, of course, get none of the personal assistance and instant gratification of the in-store experience.

Mark's antique bottle drying rack, an ingenious way of displaying your favorite empty bottles.

163

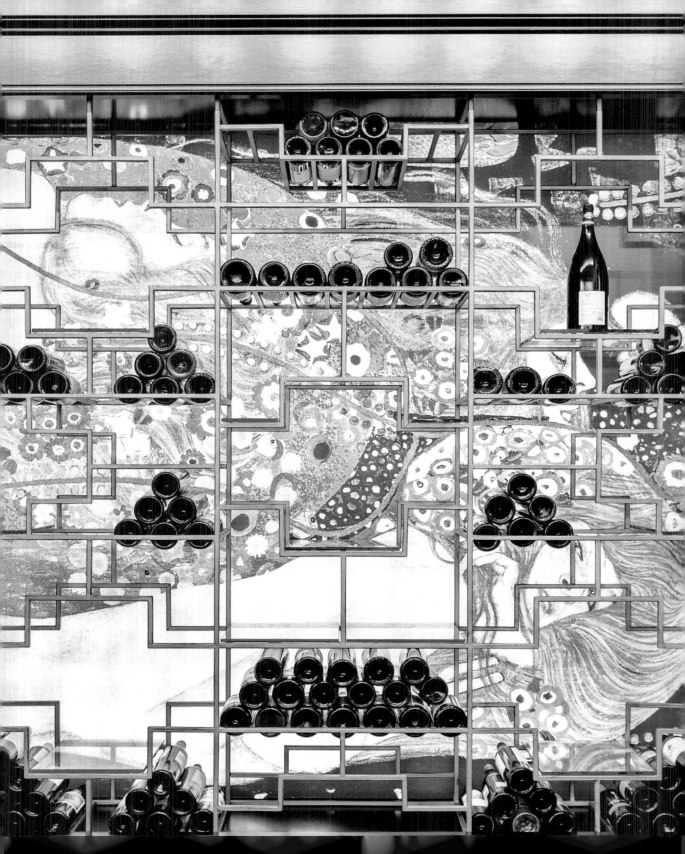

84 HOW TO TELL IF A WINE SHOP HAS A CORRUPT HEART

The quality of a wine shop is not just indicated by the breadth of its selection or the congeniality of its staff. Here is how to read between the lines:

WINE TEMPERATURE:

The single greatest sign of a problematic wine shop are bottles that are not cool to the touch. Feel a few like a nurse would palm a patient's forehead. If it is room temperature or warmer, it is likely on the road to spoilage. Also be sure that most of the bottles are stored on their sides so that their corks stay in contact with wine and do not dry out.

THE UPSELL:

Like a sommelier out for the upsell, the store clerk who blithely glosses over your budget is not to be trusted. The direction of the sale—whether it's angling up or down—is a revealing indicator of a shop's integrity.

OVERRELIANCE ON NUMERICAL RATINGS:

Stores that focus solely on professional scores to describe their wines are taking the lazy way out, as are shops that rely on shelf talkers, the canned signs written by a winery's marketing department. Much more helpful are the merchants who write personal descriptions of why they love a particular wine, not unlike the staff picks of a trustworthy independent bookstore.

STAFF RATINGS MINGLED WITH PRO SCORES:

Another eyebrow raiser is when shops mix in their own scores with those of the professional critics, as if they carried equal weight and impartiality. While some top retailers do indeed have expert-level staff, be wary of that 94 points issued by J.B. (i.e., Joe Blow, the struggling actor who will not even be working at the shop in a month's time).

NO IN-STORE TASTINGS:

In jurisdictions that permit them, in-store tastings signal a store's interest in educating and interacting with their clientele. They are an excellent way for a customer to start a discussion about his or her likes and dislikes with the staff. An absence of in-store tastings indicates a lack of customer focus.

85 PRICES BETWEEN STORES VARY MORE THAN YOU THINK

One of the most difficult tasks of a wine writer is to tell readers how much a particular wine costs. As soon as you have published what seems like an accurate price, along comes a store that deeply discounts the wine or imposes a fretfully high markup on it. This is why savvy writers know to supply only a price range and do so with a healthy disclaimer about the variability of prices.

Why are prices from store to store so surprisingly varied? The usual reasons are at play, from the seller's location (e.g., prime spot or edge of town), market power (capacity to buy and sell large lots), and labor costs (are they hiring knowledgeable wine specialists or interchangeable clerks?). It also depends on when you are seeking a particular wine, since one seller may have it on sale when another does not.

Until Wine-Searcher.com and other price comparison sites came on the scene, it was almost impossible to know if you were getting a good deal on a given wine. Now they give you an almost godlike view of the pricing landscape. All you need to do is enter in the producer, name, and year of a wine, and you receive links to wine shops around the world that stock the wine, listed by price. Wine-Searcher.com is so useful that its icon takes up residence on my smartphone's front screen. You can even check it while you are shopping, comparing the price of a particular wine, or my benchmark-of-choice "Veuve Clicquot Yellow Label," against other stores in the area or across the county.

Wine-Searcher.com is especially beneficial when you are looking to track down a sublime bottle you encountered at a restaurant or party. It is also a powerful tool when you are stalking the best price of a wine you want to buy in large quantities. Shipping costs and times vary, of course, as do a store's storage conditions, so be careful when you are purchasing expensive wine from that random Winez-R-Us in eastern Kentucky.

86 YOU CAN ACTUALLY RETURN A BAD WINE FOR A REFUND

While the process of returning wine in a restaurant is well known, few people know that you can take back a defective wine to a store. Generally speaking, you cannot return a wine just because it didn't meet your expectations—like when it is disappointingly tannic or flavorless or because it didn't taste like that luscious Malbec you had after a massage on vacation two years ago.

And if you have already finished most of the wine, you should keep that bottle to yourself. Returning it would be like devouring most of that plate of lasagna at a restaurant only to send back a sliver because you thought the dish tasted funny.

The bottle needs to be mostly full, and the wine needs to be defective. As we have seen, the most likely case for spoiled wine is when it smells of wet newspaper or moldy basement. Spoilage is also commonly signaled by wine that smells flat and prunelike, evidence of wine that has been exposed to excessive heat or a bad cork seal (i.e., "cooked").

Be advised that there is no guarantee that a seller will refund or replace the bottle, but most reputable retailers play fair when presented with the evidence and a receipt. This is doubly so if they actually recommended the bottle to you and the purchase was made relatively recently; the case is more difficult if the bottle sat in your closet for five years before you opened it.

Finally, don't worry that you are preventing that struggling mom-and-pop merchant from paying their next rent bill: they can typically pass the cost of a defective wine back to the producer.

ANNÉE 2006

THE
WINE SPOUSE

NO. <u>0010</u>

Mise en Bouteille au Domaine

13% ALC. BY VOL   PRODUCT OF NEW YORK   750 ML

87 CULTIVATE A WINE SPOUSE

Good wine merchants were once for me a wasted opportunity. I would show up, ask for a recommendation, and vanish into the ether with my bottle. These one-night stands continued until I realized that the best wine shops have a surplus of passionate, trustworthy people who want to be your vinous confidant.

Smart wine consumers therefore need to find themselves what I call a "wine spouse." Like a workplace wife or husband who provides comfort and guidance at the office, a wine spouse is a knowledgeable, helpful salesperson with whom you engage in an ongoing relationship. A wine spouse is there to gain an understanding of your likes and dislikes, helping to nurture a growing passion for wine.

But how do you recognize a good one?

PERSONAL RAPPORT:

Start a conversation with a sales associate. Is that person patient and easy to converse with? Are they a good match for your level of wine knowledge? Do they listen?

SINCERE PASSION FOR WINE:

Are they enthusiastic about wine beyond the transaction at hand? Have they visited major wine regions? Are they studying for or have they received an advanced certification, such as a Certified Specialist of Wine or Wine & Spirit Education Trust diploma?

LONGEVITY:

How long have they worked for the store and generally in wine sales? Are they making wine a career? A good wine spouse will be there for you in the long term.

THE DOWNSELL:

Do they happily try to persuade you to spend less? If so, this is another sign that they are genuine and that they have the long view in mind.

TASTE:

Are their preferences similar to yours? If you have an interest in high-powered Californian Zinfandel or svelte Loire reds, is that something that they share or at least can relate to?

SCORES:

Are they obsessed with numerical ratings, quoting digits like a track coach, or does your would-be partner-in-wine think for themselves?

88 HOW TO RELATE TO A WINE SPOUSE

Your initial discussions with a wine spouse should be about which wines have moved you. Were they white, red, or bubbly? Light-bodied or big and rich? From any particular regions? What is your typical price range? Don't hold back: a good wine spouse does not judge. Are there other wine features such as citrus or soft tannins that you find yourself gravitating to?

Sometimes it is easier to talk about what you don't like. Was that Chianti last week too bitter or the Chardonnay obtrusively oaky? Text your wine spouse a photo of the label. Create a folder on your device to save the photos of your likes and dislikes, or use a wine-scanning app to do it.

The wine spouse is also a terrific sounding board for what to pair with particular kinds of food. Text your partner-in-wine and they may recommend a perfect partner for your dim sum or rack of lamb. Need wine for a special occasion such as Thanksgiving or a wedding? Your partner-in-wine will be there to guide you. If they are on the ball, they will also alert you to in-store tastings and other happenings, including local festivals and tastings.

As the trust between you grows, you can get your wine spouse to truly help you drink like an insider. He or she will nudge you a bit beyond your vinous comfort zone. Before long you might be trying that microscopically produced Oregon Pinot Noir or that inexpensive, refreshing Muscadet that—who knew?—comes in big, beautiful magnums.

Here is a Jedi-level maneuver: ask your wine spouse which bottles are the hardest for the store to come by, the ones in short supply that are a pain to stock. Low-production wines tend to be interesting, and not all of them are costly. The wine lover's brass ring is to have early knowledge of an emerging winery that yields quality wine in tiny quantities.

What if you don't live near a top merchant, the kind where you would want to find a wine spouse? You can establish such a connection when you are visiting a top store in a wine-friendly city such as New York or Seattle. Assuming state shipping laws cooperate, a long-distance relationship with a wine spouse is totally workable.

As is, dare I write it, polygamy. There's no reason to limit yourself to one spouse. Especially where different wine shops offer unique specializations, such as a focus on small producers or Italian wine. Remember: it pays to be loose with your affections.

Some bottles deserve a cuddle.

POINTS
AND
CRITICS

NO. <u>0011</u>

Mise en Bouteille au Domaine

13% ALC. BY VOL   **PRODUCT OF NEW YORK**   750 ML

89 DON'T IGNORE WINE REVIEWS, BUT BEWARE THEIR LIMITATIONS

There are those who closely follow a wine critic because they understandably lack the time or training to judge a wide array of wines. Conversely, there are those who dismiss ratings and reviews because they rightly see them as biased in favor of one person's palate or, more dubiously, rendered in favor of the amount of advertising on the page or press junkets being offered. Moreover, it is hard to argue with the arbitrariness and false precision of the typical 100-point rating scale. Influential critics have admitted that they would not be able to give the same score to the same wine tasted on different occasions. And it is well documented that two credible reviewers can give highly divergent scores on the same wine, one issuing a gushing 94, for example, while the other doles out a punitive 81.

When the smoke clears, the best path for consumers is to take the middle ground: go ahead and use critical evaluations but understand their limitations. Or as Ronald Reagan once said about dealing with the Soviet Union: trust but verify. In other words, it is fine to trust a wine critic's assessments if you verify that he or she has a reputation for integrity. Does the critic have a distinguished track record? Or is he or she little more than a shop clerk or dabbling blogger? Does the critic have a particular bias toward a certain style of wine (e.g., big, rich "Parker bombs," artisanal producers, natural wine) and does that propensity match your own inclinations?

It also matters how the evaluation is given: as a score, tasting note, or both. A rating without a write-up is virtually meaningless, like the lazy professor who gives a paper a B without explanatory comments. Numbers can serve as time-saving shorthand for an overall impression, but they need to be accompanied by words that justify and expand upon the score.

Even if it is trustworthy and rendered in sufficient detail, never forget that a critic's evaluation is merely a snapshot of that wine and his or her impressions of it at one moment in time. Much depends on where the wine falls in the context of the other wines considered, and even seemingly trivial things like the critic's mood and what he or she ate that day. Like a college admissions officer evaluating a mountain of applications, the wine critic is making a judgment often with insufficient time amid a tiring process that inevitably dulls the senses and warps perception.

90 BREAK THE 90-POINT BARRIER, DOWNWARD

Acritic's score and review can be a useful data point in your quest for delicious wine. Because the vast majority of critics use the overbroad 100-point system, from *Wine Spectator* and *Wine Enthusiast* to Allen Meadows (Burghound.com) and Stephen Tanzer (International Wine Cellar), it is important to resist attaching too much meaning to hair-thin point differences. They are about as meaningful as comparing similarly ranked colleges in the infamous *U.S. News & World Report* survey. Instead, pay notice to larger gaps—such as that 83 versus a 92—if you want to separate the serviceable from the special.

There is, however, a small difference that you can use to your advantage, and that is the psychological barrier between 89 and 90. Gravitating to wines scored 90 and above like moths to the flame, consumers mistakenly assume that all the

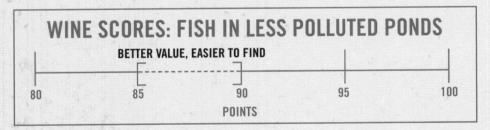

good stuff happens up there. This instinct must get imprinted on us from an early age, when the junior achiever does everything in his or her power to get that B+ to an A−. The A student gets all the glory—how many bumper stickers do you see bragging that a kid is a B student?

Retailers have long confirmed that a 91 from Parker or *Wine Spectator* moves inventory; wines that hurdle 95 create an even more frenzied level of consumptive lust, no matter that scores have generally, like grades at Princeton, suffered their own inflation over the years. Search the inventory of some online stores and of the ones that include critical scores: some don't even list wines that are rated 89 and below.

Your mission, then, is to fish in less polluted ponds: dare below 90 points, focusing your attention on the wines rated between 85 and 89 points. Not only do these selections tend to be better deals, but they are usually available in greater supply, neglected as they are by point grabbers. For value and adventure, remember the title of VH1's music show: *I love the 80s.*

91 THE LOWER SCORING WINE CAN BE THE BETTER CHOICE

Beyond the economic advantage of focusing your purchasing on more modestly scoring wine, there are other reasons to consider such a strategy. One rationale is that certain types of wine, especially the interesting, less familiar types, tend to receive lower overall scores from wine critics. Whether conscious of it or not, many reviewers have a bias for the most prestigious grapes and regions. For example, a less heralded Languedoc from France can be just as delicious as a wine from the famous Cabernet Sauvignon grape, but Cabernet is going to get a boost from some reviewers just for being Cabernet. It is like art: an oil painting and a fine art photograph can have equal visual appeal, but the former will be held in higher esteem because it is considered a more prestigious art form.

Another reason a lower-ranked wine may be preferable is because overachievers are not always built for immediate pleasure. Those 96-point Barolos or California Cabernets may have gum-searing tannins to start but are projected to diminish later. The market is replete with prestigious bottles that do not show their best at release but hopefully will do so after a decade or so when their harshness diminishes. Conversely, that lower-scoring wine may have been graded so in part because it doesn't have the high tannins and acidity that make it age-worthy but nonetheless is perfectly drinkable right now.

Finally, the lower-ranked bottle may just taste better to you. Certain hyped-up bottles can alienate the drinker with unusual aromas and tastes—such as a doo-doo earthiness or a roadkill gaminess in certain European wines—that are a discomforting change from more straightforward, everyday types of wine. Sometimes a higher-regarded but funky wine is like that kooky painting or that Michelin three-star sweetbread meat loaf with embryonic egg foam. It requires too much contemplation and rationalization when all you really wanted was the wine equivalent of a juicy roasted chicken.

In addition to being mindful of the potential value of lower-scoring wine, you should pay attention to high-scoring wines from less heralded regions. These overachieving underdogs—such as a 92-rated white from Virginia or 91-scoring red from Puglia—can be a particularly good value. They have fought the odds, and critics' biases, to make it to the winner's circle yet are reasonably priced because of their regions' uncelebrated pedigrees.

92 THE BEST JUDGE ISN'T YOU, OR THEM, BUT THE MÉNAGE À TROIS

Right now, around the world, clacking like a million locusts in heat are well-meaning industry types advising novices to "just drink what you like" with the earnestness of a self-help expert.

This would be fine advice except that we often do not know what we like, or what we like is confined to our own limited experiences. When it comes to choosing wine, we need to revise that tired old exhortation to reflect the realities of today's dauntingly diverse market and technological opportunities.

We have covered how professional evaluations can provide useful guidance if you choose your critics carefully and accept the limitations of the process. The critic need not be a nationally known expert; a wine merchant who really knows her stuff can be invaluable, as well as the "wine spouse" relationship you develop with her (chapter 87).

Today, we also have at our disposal a powerful adjunct to the critical review: technological access to the vox populi. Online sites like CellarTracker.com and photo-recognition apps such as Delectable and Vivino present an easy way to search the likes and dislikes of large numbers of passionate amateurs and professionals. Some experts disdain these aggregations of reviews as erratic, uninformed, and potentially overwhelming, but I find that if you follow the right people and don't take any one piece of information as gospel, these websites and apps can provide more data points for discovering which wines are producing the oohs and aahs.

So my advice is this: by paying heed to helpful critics *and* using technology to survey the wisdom of the crowd, you will have more confidence in your own judgment. By reading the composite reviews of others, patterns about wines and wineries emerge and provide clues as to what wine styles correspond with your taste. You also start getting a feel for the common words that wine lovers use, however disparate they can be, making it easier to translate your impressions into words that will be effective in wine shops and restaurants.

Of course, this golden triad of data—the critic, the people, and your own judgment—is not necessary or even practical to employ for every purchase we make. But the point is to resist those who would tell you one way is always best; all three can work synergistically, creating a ménage à trois for smart purchasing.

SPECIAL PURCHASES

NO. 0012

Mise en Bouteille au Domaine

13% ALC. BY VOL PRODUCT OF NEW YORK 750 ML

93 BIG BOTTLES ARE FOR ALL

There's a misconception among some casual drinkers that large-format bottles—magnums (the equivalent of two standard bottles) and larger—are not for them. People wrongly assume that big bottles are the stretch Hummer limousine of wine: outlandishly expensive, difficult to source, and as glitzy as the disco room of the Liberace Museum. While we address the first two concerns in the next chapter, allow me to convince you against the last one here.

Rather than seeing big bottles as the province of those with aspirations to saucer-size watches, Ibiza holidays, and pet tigers, you should view those bottles like people in the industry do: as magnificent ambassadors of generosity. They send a primal message of expansiveness, the signal that one has enough supply for anyone who might be thirsty. Inherent in purchasing a large bottle is the determination to share, and the decision to share it notifies recipients that they are important enough to partake in the special bottle.

This is not to discount the theatricality of big bottles. They transfix and amaze like a water buffalo arriving on the scene. A magnum's visual impact synergistically exceeds the volume of its parts; one plus one equals more than the equivalent of two, sometimes much more.

Big bottles are also rule breakers of a kind. Countervailing the puritanical admonition to avoid excess and potential waste in what we consume, they are not the most practical purchase. Anyone who opens one is implicitly sending the mischievous message: "We're not leaving here until we try to finish this." Big bottles are not so much *for* the party; they *are* the party.

A rarely seen 18-liter bottle (i.e. a melchior) that Jordan Winery bottled custom bottled for Mark's seminars.

94 BIG BOTTLES ARE WITHIN REACH

If you are one of the many wine lovers who assume that large-format bottles are as expensive as the trophy monstrosities on display at your favorite steak house, you are missing out on an opportunity of elephantine proportions. The scintillating secret is that magnums, double magnums, and even jeroboams of moderate cost are waiting for you.

Certainly, oversize bottles of fine, age-worthy wine do lighten the wallet considerably. Collectors are willing to pay a premium for them because they are in shorter supply and because the wine they enclose matures more slowly due to their lower ratio of air to liquid. And we have established that the mere sight of them make people lose it, in a good way.

But move beyond prestige wines and you will encounter big bottles in a range of delicious flavors. Reasonably priced sparklers, Muscadet, and Chardonnay are all within reach, as are supersize manifestations of Rioja, Beaujolais cru, Côtes du Rhône, red Bordeaux, and other types. You have not lived until you've had German Riesling from a magnum, which never fails to generate gasps with its tall, slender form like that of supersonic nose cone. Then there is rosé gone jumbo, which is often so inexpensive that you can afford to purchase it in the double magnum or jeroboam. A jero in rosé is a big, pink cannon that all but launches skyrockets of joy.

Good merchants usually display at least a few varieties of oversize bottles, but because they take up space and do not fit neatly into regular wine racks (though X-shaped crates are a good solution), deeper selections of them can be found online. Start by going to major online retailers and do a search for 1.5-liter bottles or larger; then welcome yourself to the big time.

LARGE-FORMAT BOTTLE SIZES
(NONSPARKLING WINE)

Magnum	*(two bottles)*
Double magnum	*(four bottles)*
Jeroboam	*(six bottles)*
Imperiale	*(eight bottles)*
Salmanazar	*(twelve bottles)*
Balthazar	*(sixteen bottles)*
Nebuchadnezzar	*(twenty bottles)*
Melchior	*(twenty-four bottles)*

95 BUYING A MEANINGFUL VINTAGE IS NOT JUST FOR CONOISSEURS

A wine's vintage year makes each bottle the ultimate consumable Hallmark card, perfect for celebrating birthdays, anniversaries, graduations, and other grand occasions. Although the traditional birth year bottle is an illustrious bottle of first-growth Bordeaux, buying wine with a meaningful vintage is not just for well-endowed oenophiles with subterranean wine cellars.

Many people seek out vintage-year wine as a gift for a newborn. The idea is that the wine will evolve as the child does, and the recipient will consume it on his or her twenty-first birthday, graduation, or wedding day. This requires age-worthy wine, but not necessarily the likes of Mouton Rothschild or Opus One; a moderately priced Bordeaux, such as that in the cru Bourgeois category, or a mid-range Californian Cabernet, such as Louis M. Martini or Beringer, will do. Your recipient should have a place to "lay down" wine, such as a cellar or wine fridge, but in their absence, a cool corner of a dark closet will suffice. What many people don't anticipate is the fact that most age-worthy wine is kept at the winery to age a few years after the grape harvest, so by the time the wine is received it will be the recipient's third or so birthday or anniversary.

Technology, however, has made it much easier to source bottles already on the market and at maturity. I like to start by typing the vintage year into WineSearcher.com to search for bottles of that vintage at stores around the world. Again, options should exist that won't necessarily empty your pocket—especially if you scan for older Rioja and Priorat from Spain; less exalted Brunellos, Barolo, and Barbaresco from Italy; or even mature Rieslings from Germany. Given their relative neglect, dessert wines such as vintage Port and Sauternes can also be found at fair prices, with even better values found in Madeira from Portugal and Rivesaltes from France. Just be sure to do your homework: some vintage years are better than others, and some dessert wines and vintage Champagne weren't made in certain years.

Other fruitful places to look for older vintages are stores that specialize in mature wine such as the Rare Wine Company (*www.rarewineco.com*). If you have a specific producer in mind, you can also email the winery to see if they stock "library vintages" of their age-worthy wines.

11%

PART IX

GI

GRAN

96 SERVE CHAMPAGNE TO A NEWBORN

We hear about how French parents serve their young children a spoonful of wine in their water at dinner, a civilized tradition that is both ceremonial and meant to encourage responsible drinking later in life. But did you know there is an even more fascinating French ritual: wetting the lips of a newborn with Champagne?

I first learned of this "Champagne baptism" when Rémi Krug of Krug Champagne told me that he, like all Krugs, received "a few drops of Krug on my lips a few hours after birth and before mother's milk." Forget playing Mozart to your new arrival; *this* is the way to prepare baby for a life of good food and wine, not unlike the tradition of christening a new ship for good luck and safe travel.

So with your doctor's blessing, try offering a Champagne baptism for your own new arrival, or slide a bottle with instructions to new parents-to-be. Make sure to enlist a special-occasion cuvée of Champagne—something on the order of Salon, Roederer Cristal, or Nicolas Feuillatte's Palmes d'Or—which the father typically opens after his baby's first cry. He pours a glass for everyone in the room—family, doctor, and nurses—and dips his finger into his glass and whets his baby's lips with it. Voilà, the little one is now primed for a lifetime of discerning connoisseurship.

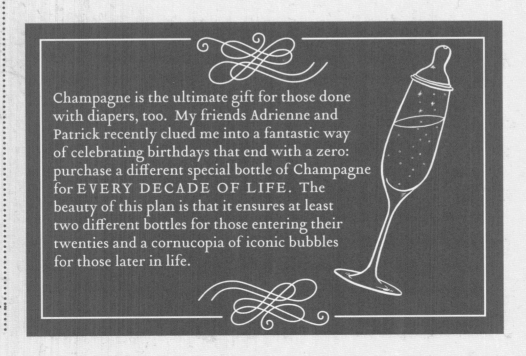

Champagne is the ultimate gift for those done with diapers, too. My friends Adrienne and Patrick recently clued me into a fantastic way of celebrating birthdays that end with a zero: purchase a different special bottle of Champagne for EVERY DECADE OF LIFE. The beauty of this plan is that it ensures at least two different bottles for those entering their twenties and a cornucopia of iconic bubbles for those later in life.

97 THE BEST WEDDING GIFT IS NAMED FOR A GUN

At first blush, a wedding gift named after a rapid-fire, battlefield gun would seem an unlikely talisman for a future of marital harmony. But the French 75 is not named for its appetite for destruction as much as it is for its zesty potency—the mixture of gin, Champagne, sugar, and lemon juice possessing the same stopping power as that of the French 75-millimeter field gun used in World War I.

Beyond the obvious—that is, what recently betrothed couple couldn't use a stiff drink?—the French 75 has a number of benefits that make it my wedding present of choice. Its inclusion of both gin (or bourbon as a common alternative) and Champagne allows the giver some creativity in choosing both special spirits and bubbly. At the same time, its relatively few number of ingredients makes it easy for the giver to assemble and an easy drink for the couple to be. Just make sure to include the recipe below in their gift box.

The creation of a French 75 is also scalable in that when an extra-generous gift is in order, you can add a pair of Champagne flutes, the traditional vessel for this drink, and even a stylish ice shaker. The beauty of such an assemblage is that if they don't cotton to the taste of the actual drink, the newlyweds are still left with a great bottle of gin and Champagne and, if you include them, the flutes and shaker. Who wouldn't be ready for battle with that artillery?

FRENCH 75

1 oz. gin
1 oz. simple syrup
¾ oz. lemon juice
3 oz. Champagne (or any bubbly)

Combine ingredients in a shaker with ice. Shake and pour into a chilled Champagne glass. Top with Champagne, and, if you wish, garnish with a twist of lemon.

---

98 THE BEST HOST GIFT IS NOT WINE

A bottle of wine to thank a host has all the imagination of cranking Aretha Franklin's "Respect" at the end of a wedding reception: safe but punishingly predictable. When you are ready to diversify your generosity, there is a solution that demonstrates just the right kind of libational creativity: artisanal Bloody Mary mix.

Not long ago, a veritable explosion of small-batch Bloody Mary mixes emerged on the market. Some are unabashedly spicy, while others are as mild as a V8. In the latter category, I have had success with RIPE San Maranon Bloody Mary Bar Juice. Many have a dominant flavor, such as garlic, horseradish, or celery salt. For the daring, there are mixes with beef broth or pickle brine, including the invigorating, brine-infused McClure's Spicy Bloody Mary Mixer.

Bloody Mary mix also offers the same advantage as my beloved French 75 recipe (chapter 97): scalability. For extra-generous hosts, you can transform a bottle of $12 Bloody Mary mix into a full-fledged Bloody Mary bin, complete with a bottle of special vodka, appropriate glasses (juice or high ball), and gourmet salt for the rims.

Bloody Mary mix is also a logical choice for wine lovers. What better way to recover from a night of vinous indulgence than to shift gears into the stomach-settling, electrolyte-infusing, possibly hangover-healing effect of a morning-after Bloody Mary?

99 GIFT-WORTHY WINES THAT SEEM MORE EXPENSIVE THAN THEY ARE

I organize my wine gift giving along a grid we will call the Oldman gift matrix, in which the vertical axis ranges from affordable to expensive, while the horizontal access goes from perceived cheap to perceived expensive.

We can immediately eliminate the upper-left quadrant (expensive and perceived cheap), which is always a mistake. It includes fine versions of Chianti, Soave, most dessert wines, and more (chapter 79). The upper-right quadrant (expensive and perceived expensive) is for rarefied celebrations and includes Champagne, first-growth Bordeaux, famous Napa Cabernet, Barolo, and other bottled trophies. The lower-left quadrant (cheap and perceived cheap) is reserved for former bad bosses, sadistic dentists, and others in your life deserving of passive-aggressive gratitude.

This leaves the lower-right quadrant as our sweet spot: the wonderful circumstance of wine that is inexpensive but perceived expensive. This happy valley includes a broad swathe of bubbly, especially the various non-Champagne sparklers in the Crémant category, which manage the trifecta of looking expensive, tasting delicious, and calming the wallet. Roederer Estate Brut, Gruet Brut from New Mexico (but owned by French expatriates), and Segura Viudas Aria Brut (with its silvery metal crest) are three key picks.

Other wines that drink and dress above their price include Muscadet, the oyster-worshipping white from France's Loire Valley, which often carries an old-fashioned, aristocratic-looking label; Beaujolais cru is another winner in both respects, its packaging prominently displaying a Beaujolais cru village, such as the chichi-sounding Morgon and Brouilly, rather than emphasizing the overall region of Beaujolais, which often gets confused with much-maligned Beaujolais Nouveau. Moderately priced Bordeaux such as Chateau Talbot, Château Greysac, and Château Gloria also offer cachet for less, with elegant labels featuring noble châteaus and coats of arms. Another dependable deal, Rioja from Spain, can have impressively gothic labels and sometimes a wrapping of gold fishnet mesh, which was historically a feature to prevent counterfeiting but now adds a dose of gilded glamour.

Embossed bottles of wine are another solution. While expensive types such as Châteauneuf-du-Pape or Napa (e.g., Joseph Phelps and Patz & Hall) may come to mind, there are several good French types of moderate cost that shine off the shelf with their embossed glass. Look for Gigondas and Vacqueyras from the southern Rhône (featuring papal insignia), as well as certain wines from Muscadet and from eastern France, like Jura and Savoie.

Any of the options above in large format (chapter 94) will increase its perceived value even more. Nothing generates glee like a towering bottle of wine, and magnums are increasingly available for relatively humble wine like Muscadet and Beaujolais.

Another way to lend illustriousness to your bottle is to deliver it in a wooden box, available at finer wine merchants and homeware stores; a gift wine encased this way is like adding a beautiful frame to an otherwise humble artwork.

Finally, consider personally labeling gift bottles with a tag that suggests food pairings or a cheeky "drink-by" date; a little bit of handwritten effort glows brightly in the digital era.

MARK'S GIFT MATRIX

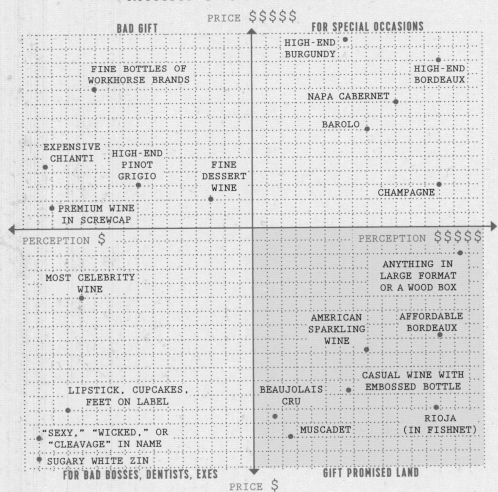

BAD GIFT   PRICE $$$$$ FOR SPECIAL OCCASIONS

HIGH-END BURGUNDY

FINE BOTTLES OF WORKHORSE BRANDS

HIGH-END BORDEAUX

NAPA CABERNET

BAROLO

EXPENSIVE CHIANTI   HIGH-END PINOT GRIGIO   FINE DESSERT WINE

CHAMPAGNE

PREMIUM WINE IN SCREWCAP

PERCEPTION $ PERCEPTION $$$$$

ANYTHING IN LARGE FORMAT OR A WOOD BOX

MOST CELEBRITY WINE

AMERICAN SPARKLING WINE   AFFORDABLE BORDEAUX

CASUAL WINE WITH EMBOSSED BOTTLE

LIPSTICK, CUPCAKES, FEET ON LABEL   BEAUJOLAIS CRU

RIOJA (IN FISHNET)

"SEXY," "WICKED," OR "CLEAVAGE" IN NAME   MUSCADET

SUGARY WHITE ZIN

FOR BAD BOSSES, DENTISTS, EXES   PRICE $ GIFT PROMISED LAND

100 GREAT WINES NEVER TO GIVE AS A GIFT

Most people know enough not to arrive at a party packing a drugstore wine, unless, of course, it can safely dissolve into the anonymity of a wine pile. But there are other verboten types, particularly these perfectly good ones that are unfairly plagued by lingering reputational issues:

VICTIMS OF '70S CHARACTER ASSASINATION:

The '70s were reputationally devstating for certain Italian wine types. Incessant commercials by Italian producer Bolla (check YouTube for a giggle) convinced everyone that Soave and Valpolicella were the official wines of leisure-suited trysts. Riunite did the same with Lambrusco in its "Riunite on ice, that's nice" TV spots, hawking its sweet, commercial version of this otherwise respectable bubbly red from Italy. Save the small-batch, dry, fizzy, food-fabulous Lambruscos now available for yourself. Chianti had its own gawky '70s phase, when the wine was orange-tinted, underripe, and housed in straw-clad bottles. Even though this prototypical Tuscan has undergone a quality renaissance and is prized for its cherry-strawberry, savory spice and food-friendly acidity, its past makes it a problematic gift.

DELUXE BOTTLINGS OF EVERYDAY BRANDS:

Workhorse wineries such as Kendall Jackson and J. Lohr make delicious, upmarket cuvées alongside their supermarket staples, but the ubiquity of their basic offerings diminishes the prestige of their special bottles. Like a Chevy supercar, they have impressive performance but lack the ability to escape their brand's blah identity.

PINOT GRIGIO:

Its invocation as a mantra on Bravo's *Real Housewives* series has made it synonymous with the image of MILFs gone wild.

DESSERT WINE:

What makes high-end dessert wine a relative value at stores and auctions makes it an unappreciated gift, because many people wrongly assume that all styles are sickly sweet.

UNGLAMOROUS PACKAGING:

If you choose carefully, delicious wine can be found under screw caps and in boxes, cans, and blue glass (evocative of the forgettable Blue Nun), but gift giving is not the time to fight the enduring biases against these types.

101 HOW TO ELIMINATE AWKWARDNESS FROM THE HOST GIFT

If you want to know how nuanced the etiquette of wine gift giving can be, consider what a French woman recently told me. She brought an excellent Châteauneuf-du-Pape to her Parisian father-in-law's dinner party but was dismayed when he did not open it at the dinner. Before his next dinner, he specifically requested that she bring some wine, which to her was the ultimate compliment in that he now seemed to trust her taste in wine. The first dinner party was an evaluation of sorts.

Who knew the simple act of giving and getting wine is freighted with such uncertainty? Time to clear it up:

GIVER:

Do not expect a host to open your bottle, unless he or she has specifically requested that you bring a bottle. He or she may have already carefully chosen the night's wines. In fact, it is best to take your host off the hook by telling them: "This is for you to enjoy another time." If you really want to open the bottle, contact the host in advance and ask if there will be an opportunity to open it. In any case, make sure to take the time to buy something special at a quality wine store, because doing so will separate you from the last-minute, liquor-store-going masses.

GETTER:

Because the bottle you receive is meant as a gift for your hospitality, you are not obligated to open it. To prevent hurt feelings, signal your intentions by adding to the invitation that you have preselected the wine, which is code for "your wine doesn't get opened." Of course, if you aren't choosing the wine in advance, it is a gracious gesture to share what your guests brought.

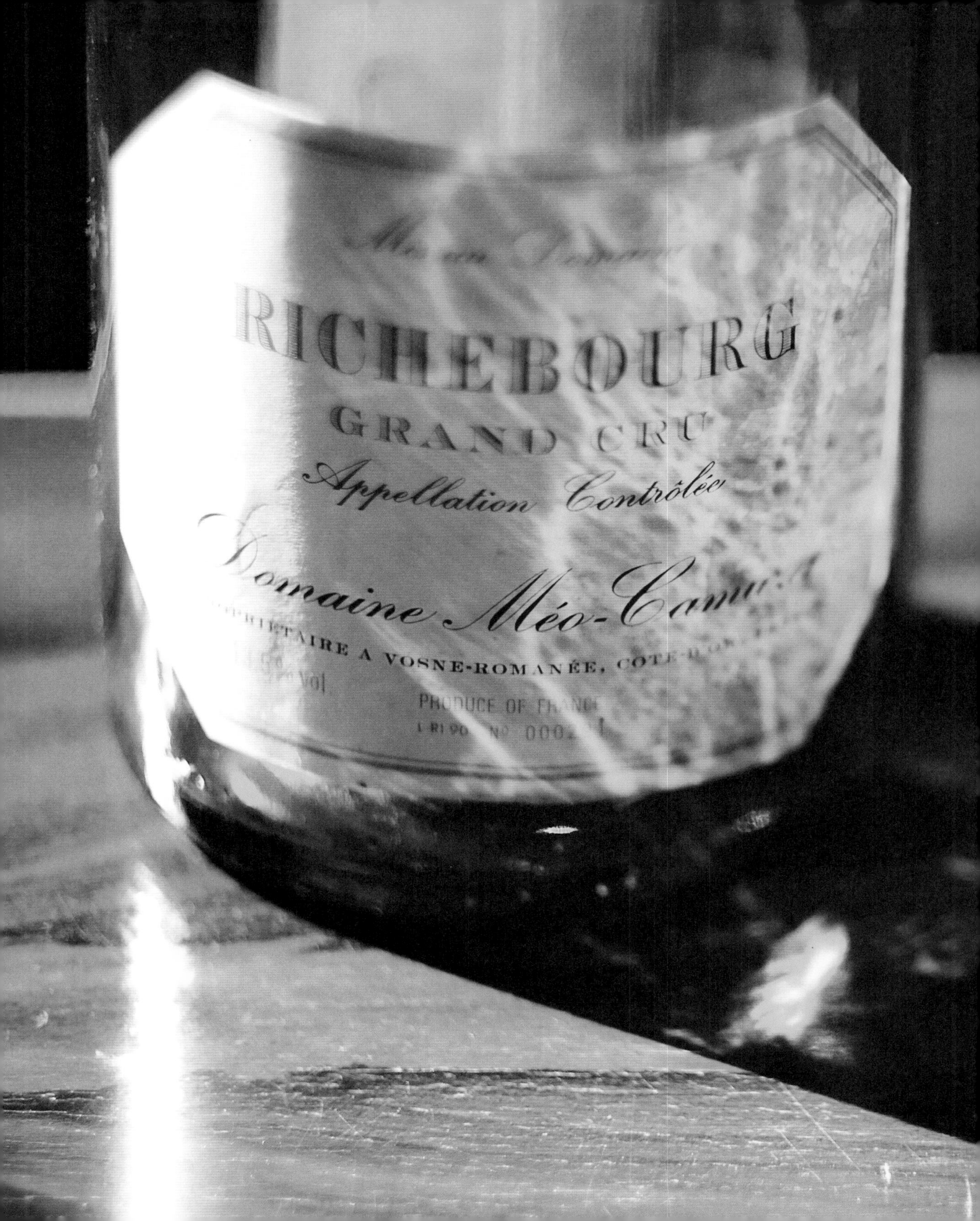
RICHEBOURG
GRAND CRU
Appellation Contrôlée

W. O.

750 ML
PRODUCT OF CALIFORNIA

1 0

R · D · S

13% ALCO. BY VOL.

102 INSIDER LINGO THEY DON'T TELL YOU

You can learn a great deal from a book's or a blog's glossary, but some words just don't often appear on official lists. These are the insider wine terms favored by oenovores, whether conscious of it or not, to signal to one another that they are in the know. My favorites are as follows:

PEOPLE

ALCOHOL AGONIST: one who zealously protests wines made in a high-alcohol style, contending that such full-throttle wine necessarily lacks nuance and drinkability (it doesn't have to; see chapter 16)

BACCHANT/E (BUH-KANT, BUH-KANT-EE): a drunken reveler. In Roman mythology, bacchantes were the female followers of the wine god Bacchus. Often clad in animal skins and toting a large staff, they are depicted in ancient art as frolicking and dancing and dashing through forests with wild, riotous abandon.

BOWL GRABBER: a drinker who holds his or her wineglass by the bowl instead of the stem. It tends to smudge the glass and kill the chill of white wine; your author sometimes qualifies as one.

CAVISTE (CAH-VEAST): "cellar master"; knowledgeable, independent merchants in Paris and elsewhere. Like the "wine spouse" (chapter 87), a caviste develops a long-term relationship with buyers and helps to broaden their horizons with carefully considered recommendations.

CHECKLIST DRINKER: those with a mission to taste the trophy-grade, iconic bottles of wine, including top red Burgundy, such as Domaine de la Romanée-Conti's La Tâche and Domaine Roumier Musigny; white Burgundy Domaine Leflaive Montrachet; Bordeaux, such as Château Latour and Chateau Petrus; Napa cult Cabernet, such as the aforementioned Screaming Eagle and others (related: "label drinker," "trophy hunter").

FLOOR PATROLLER: a sommelier who works directly with guests on the floor of a restaurant.

GARAGISTE: a small-lot vintner new on the scene and typically from humble beginnings. The original garagistes emerged in the 1990s in Bordeaux, challenging the then-conventional lean, tannic Bordeaux style with robust, fruity, less astringent wines that appealed to international tastes. Now, the term is used to describe any small-batch, unconventional winemaker, including the new guard in California (related terms are: "microchâteau" and "shedista," the latter coined by author and wine writer Jay McInerney to describe upstart winemakers in Santa Barbara, California).

GRAPE CRUSADER: preachy, strident wine pro who evangelizes about a particular wine type or style; the worst of them try to force their taste on you.

LOCAPOUR: one interested in drinking alcohol produced locally; the libational analogue to "locavore."

PINKIE LIFTER: affected, pretentious wine taster.

POINT GRABBER: a consumer who overly relies on the scores of wine critics.

TERROIR-IST: those for whom the concept of terroir—the idea that the sum of a region's soil, sun, wind, and other environmental conditions gives a particular wine a consistently identifiable character—is the all-important factor in determining the worth of a wine (also: "terroir snob").

WINE WIDOW(ER): the non-oenophilic member of a couple who suffers with his or her spouse's vinous obsession and endures lonely intervals while the seized spouse pores over wine lists at restaurants, peruses inventory at wine shops, and contemplates converting the rec room into a wine cellar

UNOFFICIAL WINE TYPES

AMPHORA WINE: wine fermented or stored in clay pots (known as amphora, qveri, or tinajas), as was done by the ancient Greeks and Romans. Adored by proponents of natural wine because terra-cotta jars eliminate the need for additives such as sulfur and represent a natural (i.e., made from the earth), non-interventionist means of nurturing wine. It is labor intensive and often produces wine that is both fresh but cloudy-looking and sometimes intriguingly intense. Winemakers around the world are experimenting with it, but it is particularly employed in the country of Georgia, Slovenia, Italy, and France.

COUGAR JUICE: insipid styles of Pinot Grigio and Chardonnay served in oversize wineglasses and favored by admirers of *The Real Housewives* and *Cougartown* (related: "mommy juice").

DEAD SOLDIERS: empty bottles saved as souvenirs. The name presumably refers to their dutiful service quenching thirst and also to the fact that their spirits, literally, have departed.

HAND-SELLS: a term for wines that require an extra effort to sell; typically less familiar types (e.g., Schiava from Italy) that a sommelier or merchant has to justify before diners will buy it. "That Zierfandler is going to be a hand-sell."

ISLAND WINE: wine made on Mediterranean islands, such as Sardinia, Corsica, Sicily, Santorini, and Crete, or the Canary Islands; a broader definition might also include islands such as Tasmania, off the Australian coast.

LIBRARY RELEASE: older vintages that a winery has stored and is now selling; an excellent, easy way to taste aged wine (also: "museum release" or "late release").

ORANGE WINE: trendy, funky white wine loved by hipster types; made like red wine with extended skin fermentation, imparting an amber (or orangey) color and sometimes a taste that is earthy and even tannic; an ancient style that has recently regained favor in Italy's Friuli region and the neighboring Slovenia. Like performance art or a Fellini movie, you want to like it more than you do.

RUDY WINE: wine counterfeited by convicted felon Rudy Kurniawan, aka "Dr. Conti." He would soak labels off old, inexpensive bottles and, in their place, affix fake labels of ultraprestigious wines. In his home, the FBI discovered a workshop dedicated to counterfeiting, including thousands of fake labels, bottles, corks, and stamps. Kurniawan is currently serving ten years in the clink.

SHIPWRECKED WINE: wine rescued from the bottom of the sea; often extremely old and able to fetch thousands of dollars at auction, primarily for the excitement of sampling a one-of-a-kind historical specimen, but often tastes no better than seawater with a tinge of fish tank and barnacle.

TEETH STAINERS: super-saturated, high-alcohol red wines such as expansive styles of Zinfandel, Cabernet Sauvignon, and Malbec.

UNICORN WINE: mythical wines lusted over by wine geeks—less a function of price than of scarcity and coolness, though all three factors do converge. Unicorns often gain their aura, like those of certain works of art, from creators who have passed away or retired, such as red Burgundy from Henri Jayer, Cornas (red wine from the northern Rhône) from Thiérry Allemand, and Champagne from Jacques Selosse.

VOLCANO WINE: wine made in the soils of a nearby volcano, such as Sicily's Mount Etna, which has garnered much attention for its uniquely minerally reds and savory whites. Other volcanically situated regions include Naples (Mount Vesuvius), Santorini, Madeira, and the Canary Islands.

LINGUISTIC WORKAROUNDS

6-PACK: reverse-snob way of denoting a grouping of six bottles; often used with prized wine.

BOJO: Beaujolais, the delicious and often-overlooked light red (page 37).

CHATEAU CARDBOARD: box wine.

CDP: Châteauneuf-du-Pape, the highly respected, spicy red from the southern Rhône Valley (page 48).

DRC: Domaine de la Romanee-Conti, Burgundy's most legendary producer and among the world's most prestigious and expensive wines.

GRUVEE: Grüner Vetliner, Austria's most famous wine (page 34).

GEWÜRZ: Gewürztraminer, the spicy, litchi-tinged wine from Alsace, France (page 35).

JERO: jeroboam, a large-format bottle that holds an equivalent of six standard bottles; uttered by insiders with gleeful enthusiasm: "Burt brought a jero!"

LA LA'S: collective term for the renowned Côte-Rôtie vineyards of La Mouline, La Landonne, and La Turque of the northern Rhône Valley. Controlled by winery E. Guigal (Ghee-GAL), they make complex, Syrah-based, single-vineyard reds that rank among the Rhône's most expensive.

MAGGY: affectionate term for a magnum, the equivalent of two standard bottles of wine.

MALO: malolactic fermentation, a winemaking process that imparts a buttery, creamy quality to wine.

OWC: original wooden case; collectors will sometimes pay a premium for wine that comes in the box in which the wine was originally packaged.

PCYM: Pierre-Yves Colin-Morey, renowned maker of white Burgundy, from simple Bourgon Blanc to rich, complex grand crus.

PÉT-NAT: pétillant-naturel, a simple and trendy style of bubbly.

SAVVIE: common slang in New Zealand and Australia for Sauvignon Blanc.

STICKIE: an Australian term for dessert wine.

POETIC

ANGEL'S SHARE: the vapor trail of Champagne that escapes when you open it, as if you were donating that portion to the spirits above; also used generally for the alcohol (such as whiskey) that naturally evaporates from oak casks during the production process.

BRAMBLY: cute but inexact descriptor for a woodsy, berry-herbal character, often used for Zinfandel and sometimes for Pinot Noir and reds from the Rhône Valley (related: "bramble-edged").

BRICKING: short for "bricking on the rim," which is when an aged red gradually turns from red to the reddish-brown color of bricks. "That Barolo showed moderate bricking."

BRIERY: vague term for edgy, spicy quality sometimes seen in Zinfandel.

FANTASY NAME: a name that the winery makes up in addition to or instead of the name of the place where the grapes are grown or the type of grape used; can carry symbolic value, or signify an inside joke. Examples include Bonny Doon's Le Cigar Volante, Napa's Opus One, and the super Tuscan called Sassicaia.

FIELD BLEND: Multiple grape varieties grown together in the same vineyard and then fermented. This contrasts with the typical and modern method of planting each grape variety in a separate vineyard. Field blends are relatively rare because of the chaos caused by different grape types ripening at different times; despite drawbacks, it is sometimes employed to give a wine more complexity and an artisanal, back-to-nature mystique, not unlike someone refusing to shave the hair down there.

GARRIGUE (GAH-REEG): mellifluous French term for *"herbes de Provence,"* that is, juniper, rosemary, and other resinous herbs. It is a scent often noticed in red wine grown near the Mediterranean coast, including the Rhône Valley. Its inexactitude makes it virtually unchallengeable and makes you sound like you wish you were Yeats.

HEROIC VITICULTURE: grape growing that happens on fearsomely difficult terrain, often super-steep slopes that are too precipitous for management by machines; not recommended for those with achy backs or a fear of heights; occurs in regions such as Spain's Ribera Sacra and Priorat, and Douro in Portugal, and the Valais area of Switzerland.

INKY: markedly dark, opaque wine, like that of balsamic vinegar; often seen in wines based on grapes such as Syrah, Mourvèdre, and grape varieties used for vintage Port. I like saying that these wines are like "peering into the inky abyss."

LACY: a term of texture used to suggest that a Champagne or white wine is light and delicate, as if woven from lace.

PALATE FATIGUE: a loss of concentration and judgment that happens when wine pros taste too many wines at one sitting; can be be staved off somewhat by frequent sips of water, nibbling crackers, and using a spittoon (a related term is: "olfactory fatigue," which can be diminished by sniffing coffee beans or even one's forearm).

RUTHERFORD DUST: airy-fairy, Fleetwood Mac–ish term for a quality some vintners notice in wines from the prestigious Rutherford area of Napa Valley. Some say it connotes a fine-grained, powdery texture often detected in the Cabernet Sauvignon from there, while others say that it's a general term for the specialness that the Rutherford terroir imparts to wine from grapes grown there. Wineries said to make wine with a Rutherford dust quality include Beaulieu Vineyards, Rubicon Estate, Quintessa, and Staglin.

SOUPÇON: twee way of conveying a trace of a certain quality in wine. It is best used to satirize wine geeks, like the movie *Sideways* did when it had the wine-obsessed Miles describe a wine "like the faintest soupçon of, like, asparagus and just a flutter of a…like a…nutty Edam cheese."

WEEPER: a wine which is leaking slightly (i.e., showing "seepage") around the cork. It is sometimes a sign of a faulty cork or improper storage.

SPATIAL

DRINKING WINDOW: an estimation of the time frame that an age-worthy wine is said to be in its prime for drinking; can span years or sometimes decades; creates angst for collectors trying to time when to drink their best stuff.

FILL LEVEL: the amount of wine in a bottle as seen through the bottle's neck. As a wine ages, some evaporation through the cork is expected, but a fill level lower than expected (e.g., below the neck) can indicate improper storage or a deteriorating cork and thus a higher likelihood that it has spoiled. Shorten it to "fill" to sound unimpeachably erudite: "That Haut-Brion had an impeccably high fill."

LENGTH: the persistence of a wine's aftertaste. "That Cabernet is wine of unbelievable length" (modifiers: "short," "persistent," "enduring," "eternal").

MONOPOLE: elegant French term for a vineyard controlled by one winery rather than shared by several producers, as is often the case in Burgundy. The famous vineyard La Tâche is a monopole of the winery Domain Romanee-Conti.

TASTING, HORIZONTAL: comparing wines from the same year across multiple producers, done to compare and contrast winemaker styles. It is usually limited to one narrow category of wine (e.g., Californian Pinot Noir from 2012).

TASTING, VERTICAL: comparing one producer's wine across multiple years (e.g., the Ridge Montebello Cabernet Sauvignon from 2007 to 2012); done to notice how the weather and vintage-related factors affected the wine in different years.

VERBS

ALLOCATE: how an elite winery doles out its best wine to favored stores and restaurants. To get their hands on "allocated wine," somms and merchants often have to agree to buy some of the winery's less exalted wine.

EVOLVE: how a wine changes in your glass after your pour it, or how an ageable wine progresses through the years.

LAY DOWN: to cellar or age bottles of wine; stored wine should be kept horizontal so the wine stays in contact with the cork and a bottle's cork is kept from drying out.

SHOW: how a wine tastes or is drinking at a particular tasting; it can "show" well or poorly.

THROW: when a wine sheds clumpy deposits as it ages, it is said to "throw" or "throw off" sediment.

TURN: a wine that has gone bad or lost its vitality. "That Cabernet has turned."

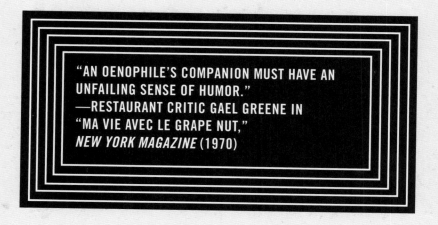

"AN OENOPHILE'S COMPANION MUST HAVE AN UNFAILING SENSE OF HUMOR."
—RESTAURANT CRITIC GAEL GREENE IN "MA VIE AVEC LE GRAPE NUT," *NEW YORK MAGAZINE* (1970)

PLASTIC SURGERY VS. WINE
FACE-OFF

TERM	PLASTIC SURGERY	WINE
ANESTHESIA	Something Endured	Something Sought
CUT	What the Surgeon Does	Sensation Nice Acidity Makes (E.g., Wine Has "Good Cut")
FLABBY	Unpleasantly Soft Flesh	Unpleasantly Soft Taste
FLESHY	A Patient With a Lot of Body	A Wine With a Lot of Body
GOOD LENGTH	Penile Implant Patients Seek It From the Surgery's Outcome	Winos Seek It in Aftertaste
GRAFT	Done to Enhance Skin	Done to Enhance Vines
GRAVITY	Enemy of Patients	Friend Of Winemakers Who Want To Move Wine More Gently (i.e., Gravity Flow Winemaking)
LIFT	Aesthetic Elevation Made to Saggy Body Parts	Acidic Elevation Tasted in Crisp Wine Like Bubbly
LIPOSUCTION	How the Vain Suck Fat	How the Vain Suck Wine
-OX (FLAW-RELATED)	Botox Fixes Flaws	Premox Is a Flaw (Short for Premature Oxidation, Which Can Affect White Burgundy and Other Wine)
PORT-WINE STAIN	Type Of Birthmark	Type Of Joy Mark
SCALPEL-PRECISE	Doctor Doesn't Have the Shakes	Flavors Aren't Vague, But Distinct
SELECTIVE PRUNING	Why Some Get Surgery	How Winemakers Get Lower Yields (e.g., Removing Different Parts of the Vine)
WELL CHISELED	Optimal Outcome	Optimal Taste

The Dead Solider that Sent Me to Criminal Court

It began innocently enough at a dinner at Colicchio & Sons in the Meatpacking district in honor of a friend's engagement. Being a wine enthusiast, he had arranged for several special bottles for those in attendance.

A merry time was had by all, and as we exited the restaurant, I spotted one of the finished bottles, empty save for a half inch of undrinkable sediment wash, which is the guck that remains in an old bottle after it is decanted. The wine was a 1970 Chateau Palmer, a rarity whose taste was as magnificent as its striking, gold-and-black label. Its plums-and-truffle perfume and enduringly silky, savory finish is forever etched in my mind. Grape nuts like me hold on to these "dead soldiers" like a moonstruck Iroquoi would collect scalps—part keepsake, part trophy, part talisman. I scooped it up and headed outside.

In the crosswalk mere seconds later, I heard the squawk of a police siren, followed by a stern, amplified directive to move to the sidewalk. A police spotlight traced my steps as I froze and shuffled to the curb, the light blazing in my eyes as if I were an escaped convict. Is this really what happens when you don't pay your E-ZPASS? My friends – good friends that they are -- scattered like confetti. The cops drove their squad car over to me, rolled down the window, and asked what I was carrying.

An empty wine bottle, I explained, just a keepsake that I was toting home from dinner. They asked to see it, and spied the smidgen of liquid inside. They started writing me up.

"No, no, that's just sediment. It's what left after you decant a mature bottle…" My voice trailed off as I realized that this explanation was about as futile as trying to teach them the art of miming.

I stood there, resigned to perp status, until one of my friends returned to the scene and informed them that I was a wine writer. That and the fact that the bottle didn't look like typical swill must have made them realize that perhaps they were acting in error. They exited their cruiser, their manner noticeably warmer.

"Ok, so this is what you do," said one. "The summons we're issuing you requires a mandatory court appearance, but all need to do is go down to the courthouse, plead guilty, and pay a $25 fine. Nothing more. And it won't go on your record."

Grateful for this conciliatory act, I thanked them, took the summons and the offending bottle, and caught up with the rest of the group. For the rest of the night, I posed for photos with the bottle, cradling it in different positions to capture the perfect selfie. I marveled that of any time to be issued an open container summons, it happened in the rare instance in which I was packing a 40-year-old bottle of fine Bordeaux. Finally, a truly Instagrammable moment.

Then the indignation set in: why should I plead guilty? I was innocent and so was the bottle. I resolved to fight.

It took a few months for the case to wend its way through the system, but when it finally did, I was ready for court, though the venue itself was eye-opening. The courtroom was not the sleek chamber of Hollywood dramas but a dilapidated cuckoo's nest populated with the hangdog faces, scruffy denim, and tobacco reek of reckless drivers, public urinators, and the domestically violent.

When the bailiff called my name, I walked to podium, fortified with a suit, tie, and my latest book.

As indicated above, the judge needed some time to process that wine writing was actually a job, but once he did, his curiosity ran high. Do I write about the wine before or after I drink it? Am I French? What was the most amount of wine I ever drank in a day? Do I know of Night Train?

When the bailiff showed him my book, he paged through it approvingly.

"You can have it," I offered, figuring that it would be a donation to a good cause.

"No!" chided the court-assigned lawyer standing beside me. "That would be bribing the judge."

The judge's next question revealed the full extent of his affability: "How did you get to be an expert in drinking wine? I'm looking for another career. I'm going to retire."

Finally, he wanted to know which kinds of wine were most ageable. As I answered, the surreality of having to teach an extemporaneous wine lesson – not only to the judge and court staff, but also, indirectly, to my fellow accused in the room – was not lost on me.

The judge flashed me a satisfied glance, and laid down his gavel. Case dismissed, along with my liability for walking the streets with an unloaded bottle of Bordeaux.

103 SAY IT *EN FRANÇAIS*, THEN SLAM DOWN THE MIC

Gomez Addams might be speaking for all wine lovers whenever he issues his famous compliment to his gothically soigné wife, Morticia: "I just *love* it when you talk French."

The French language brings authority to winespeak and also blunts some of its floridity and awkwardness. I may bore you by likening wine to a "forest floor," but you might be intrigued by its French equivalent, "*sous bois.*" Even the word "sommelier" flows more elegantly than the stilted "wine steward." Despite the diversity of cultures now surrounding wine, French remains its perfect enunciation.

The following are my favorite Francophilic wine and drinking words, many of them lesser-known bon mots used by insiders.

<u>PREPARATION</u>

CUL SEC (KEW SECK): "Bottoms up."

DÉGUSTATEUR, DÉGUSTATRICE (DAY-GOO-STAH-TOOR, DAY-GOO-STAH-TREESE): wine taster.

ET GLOU (IG-LOO): "And glug"; slang for "Down it."

GLOU GLOU (GLOO GLOO): "glug-glug"; simple, refreshing wine (e.g., Beaujolais) that is eminently gluggable (related words are: *vin de soif* and *gouleyant,* or "gulpable").

TRINQUER (TRANK-KAY): to toast or clink; knock glass against glass (a related word is: *trinch,* which means "clink," from the name of a fine Bourgeil—i.e., Cabernet Franc—made by the Loire's Catherine and Pierre Breton).

VIEILLES VIGNES (VEE-YAY VEEN): "old vines"; vines that are generally thirty years or older and produce more concentrated grapes and thus a greater likelihood of flavorful wine (also: "VV").

VIN DE SOIF (VAN DUH SWAHF): "wine for thirst"; connotes light, refreshing wines such as Beaujolais; not about contemplation but pure unalloyed refreshment.

VIN GRIS (VAN GREE): "gray wines"; another way of saying rosé or pink wine.

APPRECIATION

ANIMALE (AHN-NEE-MAHL): a meaty, funky smell, like that of wild game, noticed in reds from southern France and elsewhere; added impact if you crinkle your nose while saying it.

BIEN ÉQUILIBRÉ (BEE-AHN EH-KEE-LEE-BRAY): "well balanced"; everything in proportion; one of the hallmarks of excellent wine.

C'EST BON ÇA (SAY BOHN SAH): "That's good!"; not specific to wine but effective for expressing unexpected delight when tasting in front of a French winemaker; extra points if you clasp your hands together in appreciation.

C'EST CANON (SAY KAH-NOHN): "That's beautiful!"; used when a wine tastes terrific.

COLLIER DE PERLES (KOHL-YAY DUH PAIR-LUH): "pearl necklace"; the ring of bubbles on the surface of a glass of Champagne (related words are: *perlage,* or "bubbles"; *mousse,* or "foam").

CRACHER (KRAH-SHAY): "to spit," which is an expert-approved way to preserve sobriety. Spitting prowess is a source of bragging rights among certain pros and can even create the assumption that one possesses wine expertise.

CRACHOIR (KRAH-SHWAR): "spittoon," or a spit bucket or cup, in which tasters spit their wine.

GOÛT DE PÉTROLE (GOO DUH PET-ROLE): "taste of gas"; common quality in Riesling (see chapter 19).

GOÛT DE GOUDRON (GOO DUH GOO-DRONG): "taste of tar"; asphaltlike aroma often found in wines such as Barolo from Italy (see chapter 105).

JUS DE PIERRE: (ZHOO DUH PEE-YARE): "rock juice"; a wine with marked minerality, especially Chablis.

LES AMOURS DE LA BOUTEILLE (LAY ZAH-MORE DUH LAH BOO-TAY): poetic way to describe the final drops of a bottle, which in parts of Europe are said to give the bearer good luck and possible other rewards (related words are: *la dernière goutte* [dair n'yare goot], or "the last drop").

NERVEUX (NAIR-VOO): "nervous"; a wine with sharply high acidity.

OEIL DE PERDRIX (UH'Y DUH PAIR-DREE): "eye of the partridge"; poetic term for the pale, salmon-y tint sometimes seen in rosé Champagne.

ONCTUOSITÉ (ONK-TOO-AH-ZEE-TAY): "unctuousness"; a pleasantly thick, oily, or smooth wine, such as a rich-style Californian Chardonnay or white wine from the Rhône Valley.

PIERRE À FUSIL (PEE-YARE AH FWEE-ZEE): "gunflint"; the steely, mineral quality experienced in high-acid whites, most notably Chablis.

SAUVAGE (SO-VAHGE): a markedly gamy or earthy quality, as in some funky reds from the Rhône Valley. It can also be used for a wine that was fermented with indigenous yeasts, or a type of sparkling wine made in an extremely dry style.

SÉDUCTEUR (SEH-DOO-TEUR): "seducer"; for a wine that tempts.

SÉVEUX (SEH-VOO): "sappy"; a rich, concentrated wine.

SOUS BOIS (SUE BWAH): "underbrush" or "forest floor"; quality evocative of mushrooms or dried leaves sometimes detected in red Burgundy and other red wine.

VELOUTÉ (VEH-LOO-TAY): "velvety"; a wine with smooth texture

VINEUX (VEE-NEW): "winey"; rich and powerful; often used to describe a richer-style Champagne, such as Krug or Bollinger.

VOLUPTÉ (VUH-LUP-TAY): "sensuously pleasurable"; used to describe the velvety, mouth-filling quality of a lush, full-bodied wine.

CONDEMNATION

BOUCHONNÉ (BOO-SHON-AYE): "corked"; a wine afflicted with cork taint.

PICRATE (PICK-RATE): awful, bitter wine; derived from the term for a salt of picric acid.

PINARD (PEE-NAHR): ordinary, humdrum wine; originally used to describe the uninspiring wine rations supplied to French soldiers during World War I.

RÂPEUX (RAH-POO): "rough"; astringent; used to describe a wine with a raspingly high level of tannins.

VINASSE (VEH-NASS): cheap, awful wine.

VIN FERME (VAN-FAIRM): "closed wine"; a wine that is closed down or not expressive in aroma and flavor.

YEUX DE CRAPAUD (YUH DUH CRAH-POE): "toad's eyes"; Champagne bubbles that are disappointingly large and ungainly.

INTOXICATION

LEVER LE COUDE (LEV-AYE LUH COOD): "bend/raise the elbow"; to drink (alcohol).

ÊTRE POMPETTE (ET-RUH POM-PET): to get tipsy or buzzed; note the rhyme in the pronunciation.

SE PRENDRE UNE CUITE (SHE PRAHN-DRAH EWN QWEET): "to get cooked"; to get drunk.

ÊTRE BOURRÉ (ET-RUH BOOR-AYE): "to be stuffed"; to be drunk.

ÊTRE BOURRÉ (ET-RUH BUHR-AYE): "to be buttered"; a play on *être bourré*; full expression is "etre beurré comme un p'tit LU," which means "to be full of butter like a little LU," or butter biscuit.

BOIRE COMME UN TROU (BHWAHR COMB UH TREW): "drinks like a hole"; for someone who drinks too much; similar to "drinks like a fish."

ÊTRE DÉCHIRÉ (ET-RUH DAY-SHEER-AYE): "to be torn apart"; to be extremely drunk, plastered.

LA GUEULE DE BOIS (LAH GOOL DEH BWAH): "wooden mouth"; dry mouth or hangover.

FASCINATION

AVINER LE VERRE (AH-VEE-NAY LUH VARE): to "get the glass drunk"; the act of priming a glass with a bit of wine to neutralize dishwasher detergent, dust, or other contaminants.

BOUZY (BOO-ZEE), DIZY (DEE-ZEE), OEUILLY (UH-EE): perfectly named villages in France's Champagne region that foreshadow the effects of drinking there—first the booze, then the dizziness, and finally an expression of hungover exasperation.

CA PISSE DRU (SAH PEACE DREW): "the thick piss"; cheeky expression not unlike "the bee's knees"; originally from Beaujolais wine growers, who say it when their grapes are ripe and bursting with juice.

C'EST COMME UN PETIT JÉSUS EN CULOTTES DE VELOURS (SAY KOHHM UH PEH-TEE ZHAY-ZOO AHN KOO-LOT DUH VELL-OOR): "It's like the baby Jesus in velvet under-wear"; old-school expression for exquisitely smooth wine (also: *Comme le bon Dieu en culotte de velours* [*"Like the good God in velvet underwear"*]).

PIPI DE CHAT (PEE-PEE DU SHA): "cat's pee"; classic acid-herbal descriptor for Sauvignon Blanc (and especially piercingly tart, cool-climate versions) that some use approvingly.

TERROIR: LOYAL TO ITS SOIL

Confused by the overused French "terroir" *(tare wahr)*? You're not alone, as there is no exact translation for it in English. I tell my students to simplify the concept by thinking of wine that expresses terroir as having a personality that reflects where it's from. Its place is reflected in the glass, or to borrow a rhyme from the rapper E-40, "It is loyal to its soil."

---

104 PROVENANCE CONFERS AUTHORITY

For drinkers who want to sound learned, there's nothing like adding provenance to your descriptor of choice. Why say "apple" when you could say "red delicious" or, even better, "Jonagold"? The more abstruse, the better, since it will be that much harder for others to challenge you.

You will notice that some wine critics regularly engage in this kind of false precision. It gives a sense that they know what they're talking about, lending authority to their pronouncements. It also is the wine critic's version of social media's "humble brag"—that is, in the guise of reporting on a wine's characteristics, they indirectly demonstrate their worldliness.

MEANINGFUL DESCRIPTOR	EMBELLISHED	WINE CRITIC
MELON	honeydew	Cavaillon melon
PLUM	Japanese plum	Damson plum
BREAD	buttered toast	pain grillé
PEPPER	black pepper	ground Malabar peppercorns
FLOWERS	rose blooms	frangipani
LEMON	lemon peel	Amalfitano lemons
CHOCOLATE	dark chocolate	bittersweet Valrhona chocolate
APPLE	Pippin apple	sliced Gravenstein apple
COFFEE	espresso	kopi luwak
TEA	Earl Grey	lapsang souchong tea
HONEY	spun honey	crystallized tupelo honey

WHEN IT ALL GETS TOO MUCH, SAY YOU TASTE "KRAKENBERRY"

Don't worry if you find yourself caught in the crossfire of pretentious winespeak. Overheated, nonsensical wine talk happens more than it should, as *Parks and Recreation*'s April Ludgate memorably demonstrated in likening a wine to "dried robin's blood, old dirty cashews, and just a hint of a robot's bathwater."

Here are two solutions to neutralize the vino babblers:

ONE—GO INACCESSIBLY EXOTIC: use one of the wine critic words in this chapter or one of these hard-to-challenge descriptors: "jackfruit," "poached Anjou pear," "shiso," "sarsaparilla," "dried persimmon."

TWO—USE A CREATURE + BERRY: Wine culture adores its overly specific berries, from the simple "black raspberry" and cartoonish "huckleberry" to the fearsomely unpronounceable "olallieberry" to the rarely experienced "gooseberry." When you just can't take it anymore, here is what you do: invoke any creature and add a berry to it, such as "Cheetahberry," "Krakenberry," or "Clintonberry." Reluctant to reveal their own ignorance, the snobs will nod approvingly.

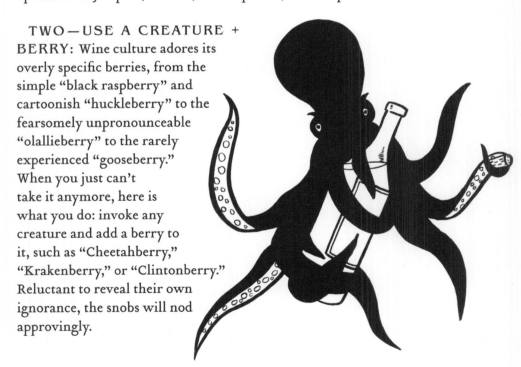

105 GOOD WINE CAN SMELL LIKE DANGER

When I recently described a remarkable white Burgundy that displayed "citrus fruits, acacia blossom, spicy oak, and a hint of sun-drenched asphalt" on Facebook, a friend understandably replied: "You had me up to asphalt. Please tell me autocorrect is to blame (wink)."

I get it: one of the things that alienates people about winespeak is terminology that seems negative but is actually meant praisingly, or at least not as negatively as it initially sounds. In wine, as in other spheres of life, a little bit of wrong can be so right. If you agree, simply use one of the words below with the following phrase construction: "This wine has an interesting [insert word] edge."

THE FACTORY

CHARCOAL: the burnt, barbecue smell sometimes seen in powerful reds such as the Rhône's Châteauneuf-du-Pape (a related word: "mesquite").

IODINE: the salty, maritime quality found in certain bottles of Champagne, Grüner Veltliner, and even some dry red wines from Mexico (a related word: "sweat").

PENCIL LEAD: the smoky Ticonderoga No. 2 scent noticed in red Bordeaux and other reds (related words: "pencil shavings" and "graphite").

PETROL: the filling station aroma seen in Riesling and especially noticeable in riper or older ones (related: "gasoline" and "that new car smell").

RUBBER: the smell of rubber tire occasionally evident in red Burgundy, Syrah-based wines, and Madeira from Portugal.

TAR: the smell of newly paved road, noticeable in certain reds from Europe such as Barolo and Nero D'Avola from Italy or wines from France's Rhône Valley (related words: "tarry," "tarlike," "asphalt").

THE FARM

BACON FAT: the smoky, meaty essence in wines such as red Burgundy, reds from Languedoc Roussillon, and Barbaresco from Italy (related words: "smoked lard").

BARNYARD: the funky manure smell (see chapter 71) considered a flaw by some but prized in restrained doses by others; sometimes found in red wines from France (e.g., Châteauneuf-du-Pape), Italy (e.g., Barolo), and Spain (e.g., Rioja); (related words: "chicken coop," "reptile house at a zoo").

BEESWAX: the honeylike smell in white wine, sometimes appreciated in Burgundy, Alsace (especially Riesling), Chenin Blanc, and the Rhône Valley (especially Hermitage Blanc).

CAT'S PEE: the acid-herbal nose of hyper-pungent styles of Sauvignon Blanc; detected in such wines as Sancerre from France and New Zealand Sauvignon Blanc. In homage to its feline zing, Kiwi producer Coopers Creek titles its Sauvignon Blanc "Cat's Pee on a Gooseberry Bush," a phrase originally coined by wine writer Oz Clarke.

FRESH-CUT GRASS: the classic fragrance of Sauvignon Blanc (related words: "freshly mown," "grassy," "herbaceous").

JALAPEÑO: the nose-flaringly herbaceous aroma associated with certain bottles of Sauvignon Blanc and the occasional cool-climate red.

LEATHER: the perfumed, woody scent of a fine old wallet, club chair, or leather-bound book; often associated with reds such as Cabernet Sauvignon and vintage Port.

LOAM: a vaguely frightening horticultural word connoting a pleasantly pungent note of dark earth, as in certain red Hermitage or Bordeaux (related words: "loamy," "crushed earthworms").

WET WOOL: the smell of animal hair or thick wool sweaters perceived in Vouvray from France and other Chenin Blanc (related words: "lanolin," and "Vaseline").

WILD GAME: the funky redolence of game meat like venison, grouse, and pheasant, sometimes detected in wines such as red Burgundy, Châteauneuf-du-Pape, and Aglianico from Italy (related words: "gamy," "musk," "aged beef," "beef jerky," "raw meat," *animale* (French), *selvatico* (Italian), " beef bullion," and "beef blood").

THE QUARRY

CIGAR BOX: the cedary, smoky aroma frequently associated with Cabernet Sauvignon and red Bordeaux (related words: "tobacco leaf").

GUNFLINT: approximates the whiff of burning gunpowder detectable in some Chablis and other steely whites.

HOT BRICKS: the crushed stone or scorched mineral smell (chapter 106) seen in Syrah-based wines and other sturdy reds (related words: "brick dust," "asphalt," "tar").

IRON: a metallic note sometimes present in wine such as Pinot Noir, Portuguese reds, and red Bordeaux (related words: "iron ore," "ferreous").

MORE

BURNT FOOD (PIE CRUST, CARAMEL, ORANGE PEEL, MOLASSES, PUDDING, CREAM, TOAST, CEDAR): a blackened quality occasionally noticeable in dessert wines such as Tawny Port, Madeira from Portugal, and Vin Santo from Italy.

LEESY: a yeasty or nutty quality from a wine's contact with lees, or dead yeast cells, after fermentation. When used judiciously, it adds complexity to white Burgundy and other oaky Chardonnay, as well as Muscadet (related words: "yeasty," "bread dough," "buttered pastry," and "marzipan").

106 PINNING DOWN MINERALITY

The first time I heard the word "minerality" was many years ago when I interviewed legendary rock musician Geddy Lee about his formidable passion for wine. He used the term to reference a pleasantly minerally smell and taste he and many others find in red Burgundy. It was not long after that I started to notice discussions about the meaning of "minerality" happening in all corners of the wine world, with critics, winemakers, and aficionados debating its exact definition with great passion.

While there are indeed several interpretations of the word, I think we can arrive at a fairly accurate sense of what most mean by it.

First and foremost, I think Geddy's impression of minerality is largely what people are talking about: a kind of minerally character or, if you will, a geology-class aroma of wet stones. I think of river rocks, a wet-quartz quality you often find in wines from Europe, especially those from France, Germany, and northern Italy.

When contemplating minerality, envision this vignette: You begin a hike in a rocky area, past ferrous stone, through the ruins of a stone church, and up near a volcano, with its lava-sculpted, molten-rock environment. You then walk down to the sea and breathe in the saline pungency of the seashore and walk over fossilized seashells. Nearby is a quarry where you take in its slatey, chalky essence. Your guide, by the way, is a military history buff, so you ask him to demonstrate his antique gun, the firing of which releases a cloud that flares your nostrils with the aroma of flint struck against steel or flint smoke or even burning gunpowder. Your trip back may take you over rain-wet pavement or sun-drenched tarmac or by a building of sunbaked bricks. At your journey's end, you arrive home having experienced the many sensations of minerality.

107 WINE LOVERS VERBALIZE THEIR SEXUAL REPRESSION

The surprising truth is that wine lovers cannot keep their minds out of the gutter. The sexualization of winespeak starts with the somatic. A wine is said to have an ample nose (smell), a full body (weight), long legs (streaks on the side of a glass), and muscular tannins (puckering bitterness). A pour of opposite intensity would be svelte, and if its tannins are soft, they can be characterized as supple. If the wine hasn't been fermented or stored in oak, it is sometimes called naked.

Things then turn overtly erotic. A smooth, rich, generously perfumed wine can be sexy, while a wine that is low in acidity and verve is sadly flaccid. A little something to grab onto is desirable, as when a fine old Burgundy is still fleshy.

One writer equated the color of a wine to the thigh of a blushing nymph. The effect of excessive oak has been called slutty or tarted up. A tropically scented, fruit-forward wine is buxom. A seductively salty taste has been likened to pheromones, the chemicals of sexual attraction.

The legendary wine writer Michael Broadbent once infamously likened a wine's aroma to that of schoolgirls' uniforms. He never went to jail.

There is also direct reference to intercourse. It is no surprise that a transcendent wine has reminded writers of good sex. If that wine had a smoky dimension, it was good sex by a campfire. A pleasantly chemically smelling wine reminded one scribe of latex sex.

Finally, perhaps the most amusing descriptor speaks to the trope of the hot cougar: the WILF.

"My signature scent is red wine. I'm sure it's always seeping from my pores. I SMELL LIKE A CABERNET." —actress Jennifer Lawrence, when asked by *Glamour* magazine to name her favorite perfume

108 OENOPHILES SECRETLY DIG THE SMELL OF DOO-DOO

The next time you see a prim oenophile in librarian's glasses, I want you to know something: there is a fair chance that they wouldn't be turned off by a whiff of poo. The dirty, if you will, little secret of wine appreciation is hereby unearthed: not all admired smells conjure the ethereal or sublime. In fact, many oenophiles tend to congregate, whether they admit it or not, by the outhouse.

Not everyone of course enjoys a whiff of manure in his or her wine. To some it is distracting or even disgusting, tantamount to slurping from the toilet bowl. But to a surprising number of wine lovers, a li'l dung in the Dolcetto adds an interesting dimension. Hard to believe? The tasting notes of some the world's great wines reference the scatological. It is the Barbaresco that is euphemistically described as barnyard or that Châteauneuf-du-Pape that conjures sweaty saddle. French writer Voltaire is said to have likened a Burgundy, not disapprovingly, to "*merde*." A famous sommelier once told me that one of her favorite wines of all time was a 1982 Bordeaux that smelled like a baby's diaper. She explained: I don't know why those smells in wine appeal to me...perhaps some deep animal instinct being awakened?"

This quality is often attributed to the yeast Brettanomyces, which for some is a flaw that overpowers a wine but for others is an element of complexity when it is subtle. Additionally, certain grapes such as Mourvèdre can make wine evocative of a dog park in August.

A regard for the excremental shouldn't be too surprising. Some of the world's delicacies—fermented herring from Sweden, Époisses cheese from France, white truffles from Italy, whole swathes of Korean food—smell foul to the uninitiated. And when you get past the initial squeamishness, you realize that earthiness speaks to the organic, to the human, to the universal—so much so that it gets its own emoji symbol.

109 "BUZZED" AND "DRUNK" CAN BE SO MUCH MORE

I used to dine periodically with a retired Stanford professor, a vibrant, cultured woman in her nineties by the name of Jane Emery. A virtuoso in the art of living, her personal credos included the gentle "love is truly listening" and the completely different flavored "good martinis, great sex." A third expression she revealed once when we were drinking Campari's and the twenty-three-year-old version of me declared that I was getting a bit buzzed.

"No, no, you're just *exhilarated*," she said, her eyes shining gleefully like the naughty rule breaker she was.

Fantastic word! I thought, and resolved at that moment to find more bon mots to describe the effects of alcohol. Evoking everything from food to celebrity to the fanciful rhythms of Dr. Seuss, here are fifty-two of my favorites for you to break out when your own exhilaration strikes:

"EXCESS on occasion is exhilarating. It prevents moderation from acquiring the deadening effect of a habit."
—playwright
W. Somerset Maugham

INDUSTRIAL: antifreezed, flusticated, rockiputerized.

CULINARY: parboiled, flambéed, feeling one's onions, french-fried, Southern-fried, tacoed, smuckered.

DOWN LOW: at peace with the floor, laughing at the carpet.

UP HIGH: elevated, playing the harp, in the ozone, seeing a flock of moons.

ANIMAL: hog-whimpered, geesed, bunnied, roostered, dipped one's beak.

CELEBRITY: Justin-Biebered, Betty-Booped, Chevy-Chased, Betty-Forded, Bacchus-Bulged, Boris-Yeltsened.

DR. SUESSIAN: zotted, zinzagged, swacked, swinnied, scrooched, sosseled, swoozled, whoozled, wam-bazzled.

BEFITTING BORAT: ploxed, banjaxed, ishkimmisked, kerschnickered, kerflummixed, vabooshed.

UNIQUE: drinkative, trousered, upholstered, amiably incandescent, vaporlocked, too free with the creature, has seen the French king.

TEXTING: :*) :S :#)

NEW GENERATION: turnt.

Drinkative WAM-BAZZLED SEEING

is-Yeltsened ZOTTED in the Ozone Playing the harp

OUTHERN-FRIED Sosseled PARE

TACOED Swacked Vapor-locked E

muckered ZINZAGGED

ERSCHNICKERED Upols Vaboos

PEACE FLOOR Banjacked Dipped one's

AUGHING TURNT CHEVY-CHASED

AT THE ARPET Hog-Whimpered Geesed R

HAS SEEN THE FR

WAM-BAZZLED SEEING A FLOCK O

in the Ozone Playing the harp Flustic

OTTED

N-FRIED Sosseled PARBOILED

PART 11

AMU

BOUC

ALC. BY VOLUME

USE-

CHES

110 ALLOW YOURSELF TO DAY-DRINK

The first time I experienced the disorienting delights of day-drinking was as a college freshman visiting Napa Valley. At lunchtime, my date and I shared a simple bottle of rosé, goat cheese, and gourmet salami on the grassy area outside V. Sattui Winery. Buzzed under blue skies, we stretched out on our picnic blanket like contented cats, gazed up at the sky, and marveled at our good fortune.

Day-drinking makes you feel like your hand is in the cookie jar of life. Although we are told that the three-martini lunch is a relic of a more reckless, Don Draper era, there is no reason not to occasionally indulge in the transportative pleasures of a glass of wine or three with lunch. Keep your mind and palate fresh with invigorating wines of high acidity and moderate alcohol, such as a Sauvignon Blanc, a rosé, or a light red. Particularly aromatic wines like Torrontés and Gewürztraminer will amplify the floral scents of the great outdoors. And bubbles are always a sound choice, whether it is the spritzy effervescence of Txakoli from Spain's Basque country or the rush of Cava or Prosecco, because they will increase the chance that you will remember your co-workers' names when and if you return to the office. Favor wines with screw caps, as this closure speeds the process and reduces the guilt of performing a dinnertime ritual in the light of day.

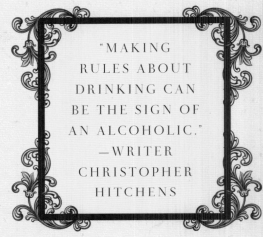

"MAKING RULES ABOUT DRINKING CAN BE THE SIGN OF AN ALCOHOLIC." —WRITER CHRISTOPHER HITCHENS

But that guilt has been diminishing every year. Legendary wine writer Michael Broadbent, for example, told me that he has long enjoyed his late-morning "elevenses" with a glass of Madeira. Musicians of every stripe have composed odes to diurnal drinking, none more popular than the recent song "Day Drinking," by the band Little Big Town, who sing that they "don't wanna wait till the sun is sinking" to indulge their thirst. Even the online branch of the Oxford English Dictionary has recently accepted the term "wine o'clock" into its official lexicon.

Fortunate are the people who come to view day-drinking as a means to occasionally create their own manifestation of *Ferris Bueller's Day Off* or, if they are recently back from a holiday, a way to extend that post-vacation feeling. If I were President, I would mandate a National Day-Drinking Day to rescue the cubicle confined. But getting day-hazy does not have to be a big deal; I was recently happy to see an elegant woman in a Paris restaurant dining solo with a half carafe of Chinon and a contented smile that said "cookie jar."

111 NO SHAME IN DRINKING ALONE

From blues baddy George Thoroughgood zooming out on lonely desert highway to "drink alone, yeah, with nobody else" to chirpy actress Mindy Kailing recently admitting in *Vanity Fair* that she sips whiskey by herself on the floor of her office every night, drinking alone has been freighted with defiance, doleful desperation, or the inevitable enrollment in a twelve-step program.

It is time to put this stigma to bed once and for all. While wine's highest calling is to promote conviviality, how gray would life be if we always had to depend on the presence of others to enjoy wine's ability to enhance and relax the mind. Solitary drinking also affords the opportunity to focus your full attention on the wine, a surprisingly enjoyable and edifying opportunity for the burgeoning oenophile.

So how best to indulge this private luxury? Half bottles are a possibility, though their limited supply makes them harder to source and a bit more expensive. A regular bottle, on the other hand, requires no extra searching and will last longer than most people think (chapter 73).

As we discussed previously, a full bottle is also your best bet when going solo in a restaurant. Not only does it allow you to circumvent the limited selection and heartless markups that come with wines by the glass, but its plentitude offers the opportunity to bestow your remaining wine on the waitstaff or another table. Such vinous magnanimousness never fails to generate goodwill, and as any philanthropist knows, the act of giving is possibly the most pleasurable part of the transaction.

112 A PORRON IS AN INSTANT MIRTH MAKER

It all started with a $10 Spanish wine bong. On my way to teach at my tenth Aspen Food & Wine Classic, I found myself on a private jet with legendary chef Jacques Pépin and former *Food & Wine* editor-in-chief Dana Cowin. In my carry-on bag, I happened to have a porron, which is a Spanish wine pitcher that I planned to show my audiences that weekend, but decided, in the moment, to pull it out along with a bottle of Dom Pérignon. Next thing you know, Dana, Jacques, and I were passing the porron around like mischievous teenagers, octogenarian Pepin splashing the bubbly into his mouth like a conquering hero.

This is the power of the porron: never has such an inexpensive piece of glassware had the ability to engender such unrestrained mirth. Popular across Spain and especially in Catalonia, the porron combines the shape of a glass decanter with the function of a watering can. You fill it with wine, tip it backward without letting your lips touch the spout, and stream it into your mouth as if it were the arced spray of a Roman fountain. It is easiest to start with the porron close to your mouth and then see how far you can pull it away without spilling. First timers tend to dribble, so dark clothes are recommended. Of course, half of the fun is watching others struggle with it, like some liquid version of karaoke. Porroning pros know how to pull back the little tankard with great flair, often competing to see who can create the longest stream without wasting a drop.

Porrons are easy to source online through Amazon and wine accessory stores. You can use any type of wine, but I favor sparkling wine, which achieves a feisty foam with all that motion going on. It is also fun to break out the good stuff with this unpretentious glass vessel, such as the Dom Pérignon we chugged before touching down in Aspen. It was a high-low combination that, after many rounds with Chef Pépin, we nicknamed Dom Porron.

113 A BREATHALYZER IS THE LIFE OF THE PARTY

On a recent trip to Montreal, I sat swaying to Brazilian samba at a neighborhood jazz club with my mom, sister, and girlfriend. As the musicians paid homage to Ipanema with their pandeiro drums and xylophone, I whipped out my own exotic instrument: a Breathalyzer, which I had purchased on a whim the week before. I had never before measured my alcohol level, so why not experiment with this gadget?

As I blew into the Breathalyzer, my tablemates looked on with amused surprise and some concern that, there in full view, I might be up to some sort of malfeasance. But when they learned that it was a Breathalyzer and saw its digital readout, they clamored to try it themselves, bossa nova be damned.

Since then I have taken my trusty Breathalyzer to countless events, and it never fails to captivate those in its path. People beg to give it a blow, fascinated not only by the rare opportunity to quantify their buzz but also by the chance to learn how close they are to the legal limit. Such enthusiasm is not surprising given the growing interest in fitness trackers and other personal-data tools.

A range of personal Breathalyzers are available online. Some fit on your keychain or plug in to your smartphone. For the foolishly brave, some even connect to apps that broadcast your results on social media.

"No drop of the divine contents is wasted, except by some newly-arrived bungler, who, by lifting up the bottom first, inundates his chin."
—RICHARD FORD, *GATHERINGS FROM SPAIN* (1864)

"[He] let the stream of wine spurt out and into his mouth, his head tipped back. When he stopped drinking and tipped the leather bottle down a few drops ran down his chin."
—ERNEST HEMINGWAY, *THE SUN ALSO RISES* (1926)

Decapitate Y

1. Protect Yourself

2. Find a Bottle of Champagne

5. Locate the Seam

Seam

Safety Gear!

Hold Bottle at 45°

Trace Blade along seam

Practice

6. Do it!

Forceful BUT Fluid Stroke

Point away from People!

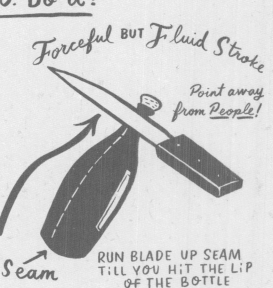

Seam

RUN BLADE UP SEAM
TILL YOU HIT THE LIP
OF THE BOTTLE

...ur Champagne

3. Make it Cold

at least
30
Minutes

4. Remove the Foil & Cage

(Point cork away from eyes)

7. Voila!!

Top portion of bottle's neck w/ cork shoots off

Careful, SHARP!

8. Celebrate!

Cheers!

114 DECAPITATE YOUR CHAMPAGNE

When I recently sabered a bottle of Champagne at the Toronto Food & Wine Festival, I split the bottle cleanly at its neck. The audience roared approvingly as the bubbly frothed up in a celebratory geyser. As I went to grab the decapitated bottle, which was wet from having been chilled in an ice bath, the bottle slipped through my fingers, and its jagged edge sliced through the tender inside of my thumb. I kept on teaching, of course, but the blood did not stop, like the elevator scene in *The Shining*. Soon fully outfitted Canadian paramedics were on the scene and went to work stopping the flow with bandages as I continued to lead the seminar.

Such is the unpredictability of sabering a bottle of bubbly. I have done it successfully hundreds of times, but because it involves so many frightening factors—contents under pressure, frothing alcohol, shattering glass, a flying projectile—you have to be ready for trouble. A practice said to have originated with Napoleon's cavalrymen, *sabrer la bouteille* is nevertheless a triumphant and crowd-pleasing way to open a bottle of bubbly.

If you dare to try it (at your own risk), I offer this tutorial:

1 PROTECT YOURSELF.
Go to a hardware store and get yourself a pair of safety glasses and safety gloves.

2 FIND A BOTTLE OF CHAMPAGNE (AMERICAN SPARKLING WINE, CAVA, OR PROSECCO can work but seem to do so less consistently).

3 GIVE THE BOTTLE TWENTY MINUTES TO GET VERY COLD, PREFERABLY IN AN ICE bucket, but a freezer will also work if you remember to retrieve the bottle before the Champagne freezes over. Note that this step is vital because the cold-ness will make the bottle more brittle and easier to saber.

4 REMOVE THE BOTTLE'S FOIL AND CAGE, BEING SURE TO POINT THE CORK AWAY from all eyes, as you never know when the cork may spontaneously erupt.

5 THERE ARE TWO FAINT SEAMS RUNNING UP THE LENGTH OF EACH BOTTLE. FIND one and take any heavy knife (it need not be a saber or machete; a chef's knife works just as well, even if it bestows less drama). Donning your safety gear and holding the bottle at a forty-five-degree angle, trace the blade along the seam in a practice motion. This will give you a feel for where you will be swiping.

6 WHEN YOU'RE READY, AND IN A DIRECTION AWAY FROM ANY ONLOOKERS OR valuable property, use a forceful but fluid stroke to run the blade flat along the seam until you hit the lip of the bottle.

7 IF YOU ARE SUCCESSFUL, THE TOP PART OF THE BOTTLE'S NECK, WITH CORK inside, will fly off. The outward force of the eruption causes any shards to blow away from the bottle, ensuring that pieces of glass do not end up in the bottle.

115 MOST EXPERTS DON'T HAVE SUPER SKILLS

When it was announced years ago that the famous wine critic Robert Parker had secured insurance for his nose, it reminded me of when crooner Tom Jones insured his chest hair, a supermodel insured her legs, and rock star David Lee Roth, during his groupie-getting heyday, got paternity insurance against unplanned parenthood. No matter the *actual* value of the feature being insured, merely announcing an unusual insurance policy is a clever way to make the world assume that you have a superpower. In truth, they will take your money for almost any reason; just ask Kim Kardashian, who allegedly got a policy on her commodious rear assets.

Some experts also like to signal that they have exceptional skills through the game of blind tasting—that is, deducing a wine's region, grape, vintage, and producer when its bottle is concealed. A source of bragging rights for wine pros and a necessary evil for those striving to pass the master sommelier exam, a blind tasting can be a useful way to hone the palate and be fun for those in the mood for a guessing game. What does not get conveyed to the wine-drinking public, however, is that even most pros are not consistently good at it, and such skills are not needed for wine smarts anymore than superior hearing is required to be a connoisseur of music. Even my winemaker friends cannot always identify their own wine in a blind tasting. Take it from the late British wine writer Harry Waugh, who when asked, "Have you ever mistaken a Bordeaux for a Burgundy?" famously replied, "Not since lunch."

So the next time people tell you that superior taste memory is a prerequisite for wine expertise, tell them to keep their sniffs to themselves. If we pros have any special advantage, it is that we taste more wines than most people and can hopefully communicate their differences with clarity and accuracy. And if we are guilty of any superpower, it is super thirst.

116 EVEN PROS ENGAGE IN THE SMUGGLE

If there is any doubt that modern society exalts the art of smuggling booze, think of all of the sleek, shiny hip flasks—some engraved, some reptile-skinned, most invariably dashing—sold at the world's most respectable stores. Since the desperate days of Prohibition to our present time, we have been a nation of alcohol concealers, with flasks coming in every conceivable shape and guise. If it can be worn or carried on your person, it has been made to hide hooch, from hollowed-out walking canes to sunscreen bottles and hairbrushes.

Many wine pros, myself included, have been known to do our own wine smuggling—*always,* it should be noted, in strict obedience of all posted laws. Some do it in defiance of alcohol markups at music festivals and sports games. Others self-provision to get a fix where none, or nothing of quality, exists. A friend smuggled a flask of Domaine Leroy Montrachet into her dear friend's funeral, which seems to me as good a place as any for a stiff drink.

I especially enjoy sneaking wine into art gallery openings, which win the award for consistently serving the world's most wretched wine. It is as if the galleries make a special effort to find the thinnest, most acrid wine to put in your glass, something that is all the more surprising given the expense of what is on the walls. But therein may be the method to this madness: like the blind man who compensates with extraordinary hearing, by ruining your taste buds, maybe gallerists hope to make the art look better.

117 BEST VESSELS FOR THE SMUGGLE

It took a visit to one of the world's most serious spas to realize how best to smuggle wine. The Massachusetts outpost of Canyon Ranch prohibits alcohol in its dining room, which seemed to me a short-sighted, almost unhealthful policy: if you are going to bother to sweat all day, shouldn't you be able to reward yourself with a glass of wine at night? Isn't that the secret to why those centenarians on Sardinia live so long?

To rectify matters, I spirited into the spa several bottles of wine, which are allowed in guest rooms. With the help of a small plastic funnel, I transferred the wine into a rinsed-out Tetra Pak for juice. This eight-sided, eco-friendly carton proved to be the perfect vessel for smuggling wine into the dining room, not only for its opacity but also for its ability to hold two-thirds of a standard wine bottle. Did I mention that its metal shell helped keep the wine chilled, and the "grape berry" label was the perfect cover in case any of the red wine spilled out?

A Tetra Pak, of course, is not mandatory for covert wine operations. A plastic soda bottle gets the job done at the local Cineplex and other casual venues, even better if the bottle has tinted plastic to camouflage the color of the wine inside. I buy these plastic bottles in bulk online and have them ready in a kitchen drawer in case my guests want to enjoy their last precious drops of wine on their way out of my place. Thoughtful is the host who sends his guests off with a doggie bottle.

118 THIRTEEN FRESH IDEAS FOR UNIQUENESS IN WINE COUNTRY

Stretch limos with neon strobe lights, mall-style parking lots, trashed bachelorette parties, tasting rooms like a Sheraton gift shop—this is the wine country version of a glass of bad Moscato. The following will help you avoid such a fate:

1 LESS IS MORE.
Planning visits to wineries is like packing for a trip: if you can resist the urge to overdo it, you are always grateful later. This is because wineries tend to close early, traveling between them often takes longer than expected, and you want to leave time for a relaxed lunch or picnic. I try to visit no more than three wineries in a day.

2 FAVOR SMALLER WINERIES.
Although highway-side wineries offer convenience and name-brand reliability, unique experiences tend to happen at out-of-the-way operations—those nestled in the hills, across the tracks, or even hidden in an industrial park. At these kinds of places, which tend to be smaller, younger, and family owned, you are more likely to pay lower tasting fees, meet a winemaker, and taste special juice. To unearth potential targets, consult a trusted merchant (see chapter 87) or a helpful sommelier. Make sure to email or call in advance to make a reservation.

3 SPIT (OR PRETEND TO DO SO).
Wine pros and other VIPs often signal their status by using the spittoons placed quietly on tasting room counters. Let the pikers chug their wine and consequently be treated like woozy day trippers. If you at least go through the motions of spitting, you'll convey a seriousness of purpose that often brings better treatment.

4 BARREL TASTE.
Short of harvesting grapes in the vineyards, nothing gets you closer to the vintner's art than sampling wine drawn via a thief—a big glass eyedropper-like extractor—straight from the barrel. A barrel tasting allows you to sequentially

taste yet-to-be-bottled wines from difference vintages, barrel types, and vine-yards. Though a privilege largely reserved for industry types, you can make it happen if your begging is persistent and your time is flexible, or if you work through industry insiders or sometimes through the winery's loyalty club.

5 BRING DOGGIE TREATS.

A secret way of maximizing the chance for preferential treatment is to tote along a bag of gourmet dog treats. In wine regions across the globe, a roving, often bandanaed dog is a source of pride for the winery. Endear yourself to the canine, and you might find yourself being poured that secret bottle hidden under the counter.

6 QUESTION LOCALS LIKE A DETECTIVE.

Look at every winery and restaurant visit as the opportunity to gain addi-tional knowledge about where the locals go. Friends are often surprised to learn that many of my favorite wine country haunts get discovered when I am already in the field and can quiz winery and restaurant staff about their top picks.

7 ASK ABOUT FUTURE STARS.

Continuing the theme of gathering intelligence, if the staff seems to be in the know, be sure to ask them about which young wineries in the region have the greatest potential. Winery staff sometimes know about the next great estate before the media does, be it a neighbor or a former employee of theirs. Even if you don't end up visiting these wineries, such questioning can clue you into a future star while its prices are still reasonable.

8 MIX IN A FEW DIVES.

The terroir of a wine region resonates deepest at the diners, pizza joints, and taco shacks that do not appear in any guidebook. These venues also offer a welcome switch-up from the intense, multicourse gastronomy prevalent in wine country.

9 PICNIC IN YOUR HOTEL.

After a long day of empurpling your lips and coating your insides, some-times the most gratifying (and only late-night) option is to creep down to your hotel's lobby lounge with local bread, cheese, and charcuterie purchased at a gourmet store earlier in the day. Pair it with a bottle picked up at a winery visit and you have *la dolce vita* at its simple best.

10 **BUY UNIQUE WINE AND MENTION YOUR INTENTION TO DO SO EARLY.**
Purchase a small-batch wine available only at the winery to expose yourself to an unusual grape or style and to avoid the regret of later seeing the same wine selling for less at your local merchant. Make sure to convey your interest in making a purchase early in the visit, because that might make the winery staff more generous with their pours.

11 **ASK FOR A FEE WAIVER.**
Many wineries will waive their tasting fee if you purchase a bottle, but some do not volunteer to do so. In that case, you should feel free to ask if they will waive the fee upon purchase. The smart ones know that such generosity has a way of engendering loyalty.

12 **CONSIDER LESS FAMOUS REGIONS.**
Though I will never turn down even a brief run through the glorious Napa Valley, smaller wine regions tend to try harder and are more likely to offer unique experiences. Worthwhile wine regions exist all over the world, but if the West Coast is in your sights, some of my favorite lesser-known areas in California include Westside Road in Sonoma's Russian River Valley, Mendocino County, Paso Robles, Lodi (nirvana for Zinfandel lovers), or the Lopmoc Wine Ghetto in western Santa Barbara County, the last of which is an industrial park of boutique winery tasting rooms. Also consider Willamette Valley in Oregon, Walla Walla in Washington State, and Baja California in Mexico.

13 **USE SHAMPOO BOTTLES TO PICNIC ON THE PLANE BACK.**
If you are flying home from wine country (or from anywhere, for that matter), follow the lead of Regina Martinelli of Sonoma's Martinelli Winery: purchase eight empty three-ounce bottles at a drugstore and use them to carry on a bottle you have acquired. On the plane order a glass of water, drink the water, and, voila, you have a cup. As Regina pointed out to me, you'll likely have enough to share with your fellow passengers, making the experience that much more memorable.

119 DON'T WAIT

The vinovores I know tend to harbor one common regret: they don't open enough of their stash.

You might think this only applies to actual billionaires in custody of cavernous cellars, but it is actually relevant to anyone who has ever received special wine as a gift or bought it on a winery visit, which is, of course, pretty much everyone. We hold on to our bottles for too long, waiting for that perfect time that never comes.

Never forget: most wine does not get better with age and that which does is far from immortal. Most of it peaks after a decade or two and then starts to fade like an old newspaper. For those who fret that they are drinking their age-worthy wine too early, mark my words: the miscalculation of drinking wine before its time always trumps the tragedy of getting to it too late or not at all. Besides, no one likes a cork tease. If you have some great wine, do us all a favor: less talk and more action. Cough it up, kemosabe.

Then, of course, we are dogged by our own impulses: our worry that we are wasting the wine on the wrong occasion or the wrong audience. To overcome such internal resistance, I recommend a simple solution: set a monthly VCD (vino carpe diem) reminder in your smartphone to seize the day for your special bottles. Those simple three letters will prod you each month to take action and use wine to *create* the special occasion that otherwise might not come. Don't stop there. When you give special wine as a gift, make sure to attach a "consume by" tag to the bottle's neck, preferably with a deadline that comes in the next year or two. The tag will make the gift twice as valuable.

The final pour is this: even if you do not buy much wine, it is all too easy to amass a surplus. The line between enthusiastic drinker and accidental hoarder is blurry; one day you wake up and you have more bottles than opportunities to drink them. Don't let this doleful fate be yours. View your bottles as invitations to heightened living, each its own vessel for joy and rapport.

REMINDERS FOR YOUR SMARTPHONE

EVERY DAY:	ONCE A WEEK:	ONCE A MONTH:	ONCE A YEAR (EARLY JANUARY):
"WINE RELAX" (TO REMEMBER TO USE A GLASS OF WINE AS RELAXING AROMATHERAPY EVERY DAY)	"BUBBLES WITH MEAL" (DRINK BUBBLY THROUGHOUT A MEAL, WHICH IS SOMETHING WE ALL FORGET TO DO)	"VCD" (VINO CARPE DIEM; DRINK A SPECIAL BOTTLE)	"BUY CHAMPAGNE" (TO TAKE ADVANTAGE OF POST-NEW YEAR'S CLOSEOUTS)

120 ELEVEN BEST PRACTICES OF THE BILLIONAIRE DRINKER

Despite the classic conception of the tweedy oenophile in possession of priceless bottles and memorized vintages, the true measure of a wine lover is in something more critical: the ability to derive pleasure from sharing. If wine isn't about largesse, why would its standard bottle contain the equivalent of five glasses? Inherent in a bottle of wine is the primal impulse to generosity.

To drink like a billionaire in full, strive always to do the following:

1 POUR FOR OTHERS BEFORE yourself.

2 WHEN YOU BYO WINE TO A restaurant, share a taste with your server and sometimes the chef.

3 WHEN YOU DINE OUT BY yourself, occasionally order a full bottle and share the remaining with the staff or an unsuspecting couple.

4 PURCHASE LARGE-FORMAT bottles such as magnums and jeroboams, which are increasingly available for moderately priced wine.

5 WHEN HOSTING A PARTY, allow for significantly more wine than the hospitality books say you need.

"IF THERE IS TO BE **CHAMPAGNE,** HAVE NO STINT OF IT... PROFUSION IS THE CHARM OF HOSPITALITY... PLUNGE INTO THE GENEROUS STREAM"
—WILLIAM THACKERAY, *BARMECIDE BANQUETS* (1845)

"YET I DON'T THINK IT *SAGE/TO ENTOMB IT,* AS SOME OF YOUR CONNOISSEURS DO/TILL IT'S LOSING IN FLAVOUR, AND BODY, AND HUE..."
—RICHARD HARRIS BARHAM, *THE INGOLDSBY LEGENDS* (1837)

6 WHEN YOU HOST A LARGER GATHERING, PREPOUR A GLASS OF WINE SO THAT people get a drink as soon as they enter your lair. Adopt a zero-waiting policy.

7 WHILE NO ONE WASTES SPECIAL WINE ON THE INDIFFERENT, AVOID "GOING NIXON" on guests who might be wine curious. (Once on the presidential yacht *Sequoia*, Richard Nixon infamously served his guests humble wine while he secretly drank Château Margaux.) The bottom line is that you never know when you may inspire the next oenophile. Err on the side of pouring your good stuff.

8 EYE YOUR GUESTS' EMPTY GLASSES LIKE A HAWK. LIKE REPLENISHING A WINTER bird feeder, your duty is to make sure they stay filled.

9 IF YOU ARE THE WINE LOVER IN YOUR HOUSEHOLD, ENSURE YOUR STASH INCLUDES a safe area that others can draw from without their having to worry about depleting your special stuff.

10 CONSIDER SENDING GUESTS OFF WITH DOGGIE BOTTLES OF LEFTOVER WINE. I keep small plastic bottles on hand just for this purpose.

11 ALWAYS REMEMBER: WINE IS A VAMPIRE SHIELD AGAINST THE VICISSITUDES OF life. Grab the chalice by its stem, and get thee to a bottle.

Acknowledgments

To Ellen Connolly, for her deluxe, solar-warm support, not the least of which included swabbing my mouth with Château d'Yquem moments before I submitted to a three-hour surgery.

To Burt McMurtry, for his extraordinary friendship and for bestowing on me a PhD in Quantum Oenophilia, and his lovely wife and bon amie, Deedee.

A HIGH RAISE OF THE CHALICE TO:

My editor, Lucas Wittmann, a gentleman of letters, acumen, and oenomania, who shared my vision from the first sip; Judith Regan, genius domus of Regan Arts and unflinching protectress of the creative act; Richard Ljoenes, maker of grand designs; Gregory Henry, publicist extraordinaire; Lynne Ciccaglione; and Emily Greenwald.

Eric Rayman, whose insight and foresight led me to Regan Arts; Angela Miller, my skillful and turophilic agent; and Nader Mousavi, champion decanter of cult Cabernet.

Lea Tucker and Megan Shean, my Aspen A-Team, always up for the next caper.

Rob Schipano, whose design talents never cease to generate glee.

A HEALTHY POUR OF GRATITUDE TO THESE AGENTS OF INSPIRATION AND INTOXICATION:

Adrian Jasso; Adrienne Jamieson and Patrick Chamorel; all Food & Wine Classic in Aspen volunteers; Alyssa Rapp; Amy Klewitz; Ana Moreno VanDiver and Pedro Gonzalez; Andrea Hazen and Edouard Mauvais-Jarvis; Antonio Francisco; Barbara Stallins, Carolyn Manning, Howard Wolf, all who oversee the Stanford Wine Collection; BCWC; Bobby and Jen Peters; Cathy McMurtry and Jim McLaughlin; Cathy Nelson and Jonathan Corl; Christina Grdovic, Diella Koberstein Allen, Devin Padgett, Ray Isle, Nilou Motamed, and all other Food & Wine Classicists; CJ Tropp; Dan Beltramo; Dane L. Neal; David Fink; Dennis Foley; Dick "Scandi Wine Savant" Christie; Dillon Cohen and Kate Holten; Dr. Barry Chaiken; Dr. Paul McCormick; Erika Seidman and Ben Downing; Evan Lodes and Laura Pei; Fred and Carol Schrader; Gail Simmons; Gillian Conway; Grace Chung; Jacques Pépin; James Corl and Krista Shulz; Jennifer DePriest; Jesse Kornbluth; Jim McMurtry; Jiyang Chen; Joe Schoendorf; John Abbott; John and Janet McMurtry; Joy Simmons; K. Don Cornwell; Kevin and Julia Hartz; Kevin Warsh and Jane Lauder; Kimberly Burns; Larry Mohr; Lee Black; Lee Schrager; Lisa Mattson; Liz and Ed Somekh; Long Nguyen; Lynn Fritz; M. Alexander Hoye; Marcus Samuelsson; Mark "El Burro" Hernandez; Marty "MJ" Higgins; Matt Oggero; Orley Ashenfelter; Peter Hellman; Rosina Miller; Samer Hamadeh and Alison Harmelin; Shelley Phillips, Dre Anderson, and all at C3 Presents; Steve Attardo; Steve Herrick; Vicki and Roger Sant; Wes Marshall; Wendy Munger; Woof dwellers

A 21-CORK SALUTE TO OLDMANS EVERYWHERE, AND ESPECIALLY MARILYN, ELLIOTT, AND ELIZABETH.

"UNHAND THAT BOTTLE!"

INDEX

Image Credits

RED HERMITAGE

MULTIBILLIONAIRE ($3,000+)
- Jean-Louis Chave Ermitage "Cuvée Cathelin"

BILLIONAIRE ($250+)
- Jean-Louis Chave Hermitage Rouge

MILLIONAIRE ($80 to $120)
- Delas Frères Hermitage "Domaine des Tourettes"
- J. L. Chave Sélections St.-Joseph Offerus
- M. Chapoutier Hermitage "Monier de la Sizeranne"

THOUSANDAIRE (under $40)
- Alain Graillot Crozes-Hermitage
- Emmanuel Darnaud Crozes-Hermitage "Les Trois Chênes"
- Jean-Luc Colombo Crozes-Hermitage "Les Fées Brunes"

You'll pay a premium for the legendary and powerful Syrah known as Hermitage, but in the right hands of fellow Northern Rhône appellation St-Joseph can spirit you pretty close to Hermitage's brooding blackberry-and-herb majesty. A step down in price and concentration is Crozes-Hermitage, considered a "baby Hermitage," able to dial up some of the Northern Rhône's dark, smoky charm.

CÔTE-RÔTIE

BILLIONAIRE ($600+)
- E. Guigal Côte-Rôtie "La Mouline"

MILLIONAIRE ($80 to $100)
- E. Guigal Côte-Rôtie "Brune et Blonde"
- Saint Cosme Côte-Rôtie
- R. Rostaing Côte-Rôtie "Ampodium"

THOUSANDAIRE (under $40)
- Domaine des Hauts Châssis Syrah "La Champine"
- Domaine Lombard Syrah "La Côte"
- R. Rostaing Syrah "Les Lézardes"

Côte-Rôtie, the famously floral, peppery, Syrah-focused red from the Rhône Valley meets its apotheosis in E. Guigal's single vineyard "La La" bottlings, but venerable producer René Rostaing can deliver similar quality with significant savings. Not only is his "Ampodium" Côte-Rôtie blended from several top parcels, but his "Les Lézardes" bottling comes from Syrah grapes grown in the Côte-Rôtie zone, which are declassified to the more general "Vin de Pays" because he deems them too young for the name Côte-Rôtie. Domaine's Lombard's excellent Vin de Pays "La Côte" is even easier on the wallet.

CHÂTEAUNEUF-DU-PAPE

BILLIONAIRE ($600 to $800)
- Château de Beaucastel Châteauneuf-du-Pape "Hommage à Jacques Perrin"

MULTIMILLIONAIRE ($120+)
- Château Rayas Châteauneuf-du-Pape
- Henri Bonneau & Fils Châteauneuf-du-Pape "Réserve des Célestins"
- Domaine du Pégau Châteauneuf-du-Pape Cuvée Réservée

MILLIONAIRE ($60 to $120)
- Château de Beaucastel
- Domaine du Vieux Télégraphe "La Crau"
- Château La Nerthe

THOUSANDAIRE (Under $50)
- Château de Beaucastel Côtes du Rhône "Coudoulet Rouge"
- E. Guigal Gigondas
- Tardieu-Laurent Vacqueyras "Vieilles Vignes"

Economical alternatives to the earthy, roasted berry deliciousness that is Southern Rhône's Châteauneuf-du-Pape are plentiful in the neighboring regions of Vacqueyras (Vah-kay-rahss) and Gigondas (Jhee-gohn-das). Even more affordable is Côtes du Rhône, which is often uncomplicated and straightforward but from a talented producer and can get you the flavor, if not some of the complexity and depth, of a CdP. Château de Beaucastel Côtes du Rhône "Coudoulet Rouge," for example, is known to insiders as a as a "baby Beaucastel Châteauneuf-du-Pape," sourced as it is from grapes next to the producer's renowned Châteauneuf-du-Pape vineyard.

NAPA VALLEY CABERNET

BILLIONAIRE ($1,000+)
- Screaming Eagle Cabernet Sauvignon

MULTIMILLIONAIRE ($200 to $500)
- Dalle Valle Maya, Scarecrow Cabernet Sauvignon
- Schrader Cellars "Old Sparky" Beckstoffer To Kalon Vineyard Cabernet Sauvignon

MILLIONAIRE: ($80 to $200)
- Hewitt Cabernet Sauvignon Rutherford
- Robert Mondavi To Kalon Vineyard Reserve Cabernet Sauvignon
- TOR Oakville Beckstoffer To Kalon Vineyard Clone No.6 Cabernet Sauvignon

THOUSANDAIRE (under $50)
- Buehler Napa Valley Estate Cabernet Sauvignon
- Newton Napa County Cabernet Sauvignon
- Villa Mt. Eden Cabernet Sauvignon Grand Reserve

Those lacking the paper to invest in the To Kalon vineyard sourced "Old Sparky" from cult cabernet house Schrader Cellars can more affordably access Napa opulence through Robert Mondavi's cuvée, which was the wine that established To Kalon as one of the world's great vineyards. In general, value in Napa cabernet is found from such low-buzz pioneers, a category so important I expand upon it in the sidebar. Stalwarts like Buehler, Newton, and Villa Mt. Eden are gloriously untrendy, and you'll pay less for that fact.

SUPER TUSCAN

BILLIONAIRE ($600+)
-Masseto

MULTIMILLIONAIRE ($200 to $400)
-Montevertine "Le Pergole Torte"
-Tenuta dell'Ornellaia "Ornellaia"
-Tenuta San Guido "Sassicaia"

MILLIONAIRE: ($75 to $120)
-Antinori "Tignanello"
-Felsina "Fontalloro"
-Tenuta dell'Ornellaia Le Serre Nuove

THOUSANDAIRE (under $35)
-Banfi Brancaia "Tre"
-Ceralti "Scirè" Bolgheri
-Tenuta dell'Ornellaia "Le Volte"

No need to operate a Ponzi scheme to lay your lips on a super Tuscan, which is the category of Italian reds that come from non-traditional grape blends and/or are grown outside the official Chianti zone of Tuscany. Le Serre Nuove is the dependably delicious second label of the famed Ornellaia, while Le Volte is its excellent third label. Brancaia "Tre," a blend of three grapes—sangiovese, merlot, and cabernet sauvignon—is perennially a steal, as is the similarly built Castello Banfi "Centine."

BAROLO AND BARBARESCO

BILLIONAIRE ($700+)
-Giacomo Conterno Barolo "Monfortino" Riserva

MULTIMILLIONAIRE: ($200 to $500)
-Angelo Gaja (GAH-yah) Barbaresco
-Bruno Giacosa "Falletto" Barolo Riserva
-Prunotto Barolo Riserva Bussia Vigna Colonnello
-Vietti (VYEHT-tee) Villero Barolo Riserva

MILLIONAIRE ($80 to $150)
-Elio Altare Barolo Cerretta
-Giacomo Borgogno & Figli Barolo Riserva
-Paitin Barbaresco Sorì Paitin
-Paolo Scavino Cannubi Barolo
-Pio Cesare Barolo Ornato

THOUSANDAIRE (Under $40)
-Cavallotto Langhe Nebbiolo
-Elio Grasso Barbera d'Alba Vigna Martina
-Paolo Scavino Barbera d'Alba
-Produttori del Barbaresco Langhe Nebbiolo

Piedmont's celebrated Barolo and its Nebbiolo-powered sister Barbaresco are wallet draining but not as punishingly pricey as their counterparts from Bordeaux and Burgundy. A solid understudy is Langhe Nebbiolo, which is a Nebbiolo-based wine from Piedmont that did not make the cut (typically because it came from younger grapes and/or less exalted vineyards) for the more expensive Barolo and Barbaresco. Another strategy is to look for the grape Barbera from a talented Piedmontese producer such as Elio Grasso or Paolo Scavino. Both cases get you "Piedmont Lite," a typically softer and less complex red that requires no bottling aging.

LOW-BUZZ PIONEERS: THE SECRET TO VALUE FOR NAPA CAB

Let others pursue the mailing list wineries that play hard to get. Billionaire flavor and complexity can be found for far less with cabernet and related blends from old school producers whose buzz has long subsided. I call these venerable wineries the Low-Buzz Pioneers (LBP). Many of them got first dibs on the best land and produce wine in relatively large quantities, both of them factors that can lead to relief at the cash register. Here are 10 compelling LBPs and their dependably excellent under Cabernet (all about $50 or less).

LBP	FOUNDED	VALUE BOTTING
BEAULIEU	1900	*Beaulieu Vineyard Rutherford Cabernet Sauvignon*
BERINGER	1897	*Beringer Knights Valley Cabernet Sauvignon*
CHAPPELLET	1967	*Chappellet Signature Napa Valley Cabernet Sauvignon*
FREEMARK ABBEY	1939	*Freemark Abbey Napa Valley Cabernet Sauvignon*
FLORA SPRINGS	1978	*Flora Springs Napa Valley Cabernet Sauvignon*
HONIG	1964	*Honig Napa Valley Cabernet Sauvignon*
LOUIS M. MARTINI	1933	*Louis M. Martini Napa Valley Cabernet Sauvignon*
RAYMOND	1970	*Raymond Napa Valley Reserve Selection Cabernet Sauvignon*
ROBERT MONDAVI	1966	*Robert Mondavi Napa Valley Cabernet Sauvignon*
TREFETHEN	1978	*Trefethen Oak Knoll District Cabernet Sauvignon*